COLLECTED
NONSENSE AND LIGHT VERSE

Gilbert Keith Chesterton (1874–1936) was one of this century's most distinguished men of letters. He was born in Kensington, London, was educated at St Paul's School, and later studied art at the Slade School and literature at University College, London.

By the time he was twenty-one, he was well launched as a reviewer and journalist. He found himself justly famous in 1905 on the publication of his book *Heretics*. A stream of essays, literary and art criticism, poetry, history and novels followed over the next thirty years.

His best-known books are *The Man Who Was Thursday*, a fantastic novel, and *The Everlasting Man*, his history of mankind's spiritual progress – and of course the Father Brown detective stories.

Methuen Humour Classics

G.K.CHESTERTON
Collected Nonsense and Light Verse

SELECTED AND ARRANGED BY

Marie Smith

A Methuen Paperback

First published in 1987
by Xanadu Publications Limited
This paperback edition published 1988
by Methuen London Ltd
11 New Fetter Lane, London EC4P 4EE
This selection and Introduction © Marie Smith 1987

Printed and bound in Great Britain by
Richard Clay Ltd, Bungay, Suffolk

British Library Cataloguing in Publication Data

Chesterton, G. K.
    Collected nonsense and light verse.
    I. Title   II. Smith, Marie
    821´.912   PR4453.C4

ISBN 0-413-18170-7

CONTENTS

INTRODUCTION

For a man whose comic verse is so well-known and loved, it is aston-
ishing that there has never been a major collection of G.K.
Chesterton's work in this vein. Poems like 'The Rolling English
Road', 'Ballade of Suicide' and 'Song Against Grocers' are classic
anthology pieces, yet they are only a handful from a life-long output,
much of which is equally good and which deserves to be far more
widely known. It was to put these matters straight that I embarked
on the task of assembling something like a definitive collection of
Chesterton's nonsense and light verse.

It was W.H. Auden who supplied the spark. In a short but very
perceptive essay he makes some valid criticisms of Chesterton's con-
ventional poetry, then moves swiftly on to enthuse about *Greybeards
at Play*, which he has just read for the first time. 'I have no hesi-
tation,' he writes, 'in saying that it contains some of the best pure
nonsense verse in English, and the author's illustrations are equally
good.' Auden also quotes stanzas from other poems, adding, 'I can-
not think of a single comic poem by Chesterton that is not a triumph-
ant success ... Surely it is high time that such enchanting pieces
should be made readily available.' I set to work with a will.

It turned out to be a voyage of discovery and one of great enjoy-
ment. I knew, of course, that Chesterton was prolific, but I was not
prepared for the mass of material that came to light once I began
searching for it, and I gladly acknowledge my debt to Chesterton's
friend and biographer, Maisie Ward, and to his bibliographer, John
Sullivan, without whose pioneering efforts my task would have been
well nigh impossible.

A brief word about my principle of selection before moving on to
the verses themselves. The book is called *Collected Nonsense and
Light Verse*. The 'Nonsense' part is straightforward enough, for I
have indeed collected all of Chesterton's known work in this idiom,
but 'Light Verse' is a broad category that ranges from near-nonsense
jingles to fairly serious poetry – and I for one will not attempt to
define it any more precisely than that. I have simply gone by the tone

of each poem, which is more a matter of personal response than anything else, preferring lesser-known and uncollected examples to those already included in the *Collected Poems*, to avoid duplicating too many of the contents of that excellent though far-from-comprehensive tome. The 'Collected' in the present title should not, therefore, be taken to mean that the assembly is in any sense complete. It includes the most celebrated of G.K. Chesterton's humorous poems and it gathers together from widely disparate sources many pieces that in my view are equally fine and much less familiar – but Chesterton was hugely prolific, a book is a finite thing, and lines have to be drawn somewhere.

The verses that are *not* here I have tended to exclude because of their now-dated topicality – Chesterton was always given to penning little verses commenting on some current news item – or because of their very specific associations with one person or one occasion. Most of these would now be fairly meaningless without detailed notes explaining who was who and what was going on, and even with the topical poems that *are* included I have tried to avoid footnotes as contrary to the spirit of the thing, except when there is a good excuse for one: the chance to include a pertinent clerihew, or an amusing drawing, for instance.

The book as a whole represents just one person's choice from a vast output, but although there may be quibbles about some of the inclusions and omissions, I am confident that by and large it does contain the best of G.K. Chesterton's humorous verse.

I AND IV   GREYBEARDS AT PLAY and BOB-UP-AND-DOWN

The pure nonsense verse is contained in these two sections of the book. Section I includes the whole of Chesterton's first published work (or the second, according to some), *Greybeards at Play*, together with a few additional verses from this period that have not been collected before. Chesterton was employed at this time as a publisher's assistant, working in his spare moments on novels and poems, and writing occasional pieces of criticism – trying to become a writer and trying also to marry his fiancée of long standing, Frances Blogg. His first two books were published in 1900 (the other was the much more serious *The Wild Knight, and Other Poems*), and they were financed by his father. There is no doubt that his hopes rested primarily on the serious poems, for he wrote in a letter to Frances: 'To publish a book of my nonsense verses seems to me exactly like summoning the whole of the people of Kensington to see me smoke cigarettes'.

As Chesterton's fame grew, the poems of *The Wild Knight* came to be incorporated in the various editions of his *Collected Poems*, but *Greybeards at Play* might never have existed as far as he was concerned, and it has been only fitfully in print since then. Perhaps this sort of writing did come too easily; he never took it seriously, and although he continued to pour it out in great abundance all through his life, it was mostly done for the amusement of friends and children. Many examples are included in Section IV of the present collection.

Does this show a sly concern for his own literary reputation, of which he was invariably dismissive elsewhere? I think not. It is more likely that he simply could not understand why people should want to bother with such froth, which – surely – anyone could have knocked off in a moment. Not so, of course.

II THE ROLLING ENGLISH ROAD

These verses, mostly from *The Flying Inn* (1914, but serialized the year before), include some of Chesterton's best-known and best-loved works, which were subsequently collected as *Wine, Water and Song*. They are mature poems from Chesterton's best period, and it is upon poems like 'The Rolling English Road', 'The Song of Quoodle' and 'Wine and Water' that his reputation as a humorous poet presently rests; they naturally occupy a prominent place in this collection.

'The Good Grocer', which closes this section of the book, is a late attempt to make amends for the original 'Song Against Grocers': nowhere near as good as that wonderful diatribe, but interesting and worth including nonetheless.

III THE WORSHIPPER'S HALF-HOLIDAY

This section brings together all of Chesterton's parodies, with which he obviously had enormous fun. There are two major groups of these. The first, 'Variations of an Air', was written for the occasion of Chesterton's appearance in the character of Old King Cole at a pageant in his home town of Beaconsfield in 1920, and the verses were published in a pamphlet which was sold to raise money for the local Children's Convalescent Home. They were later reprinted in *The New Witness* and included in the *Collected Poems*. W.H. Auden, in the essay praising Chesterton's comic verse, wrote that 'his parodies of other poets are equally good, especially those of Browning and Kipling'.

The second group comprises the 'Answers to the Poets', which appeared serially in *G.K.'s Weekly* in 1925, and these poems take things a stage further – the Skylark, for instance, replies to Wordsworth, but does so *in the style of Byron*. A delightful, if complicated, notion. These too were included in the *Collected Poems*, with the puzzling omission of 'Lady Clara Vere de Vere replies to Mr Alfred Tennyson', which is here restored. In this section I have also included a few other stray verses in this vein, together with a mock school essay tracing the history of the tomato in literature, with hilarious examples of its occurrence.

The title of this section, incidentally, is Chesterton's own definition of parody.

V   CHUCK IT, SMITH!

Probably the most scathing satirical verses since Pope, these reveal Chesterton in a rather different light and at the top of his form. On the whole, the poems explain themselves (often with a helpful quotation at the top to mark the occasion) and, even if the reader is none too familiar with the causes and personalities that Chesterton is attacking, they can be enjoyed as virtuoso performances in their own right. As I said earlier, I have no wish to burden what is essentially a light-hearted book with leaden footnotes. There is no major single source for these poems: they are scattered across thirty years of journalism.

At this distance it is easy to forget that these issues *mattered*, and that to mock F.E. Smith (the advocate, later Lord Birkenhead) or Walter Long required real courage, for these were powerful and influential men. 'The Song of Right and Wrong', in Section II of this book, cost Chesterton his lucrative and much-needed position as a columnist for *The Daily News*. The paper was owned by Mr Cadbury, whose fortune had come from cocoa and whose politics Chesterton had come to deplore. It is difficult to think of many modern journalists who would resign in so spectacular and irrevocable a fashion!

VI I THINK I WILL NOT HANG MYSELF TODAY

Only five ballades found their way into the *Collected Poems*, but with the *Flying Inn* songs they are among the most widely quoted and anthologized poems of Chesterton's entire output. Of the additional twenty-four included here one or two are occasional verses and rather slight, but the rest are of the same very high standard and their neglect is hard to understand. At any rate, here in one place for the first time are all of Chesterton's ballades that have come to light.

This old and difficult form was revived by the 'club' that wrote for the *New Witness*, whose members included Maurice Baring, E.C. Bentley and Hilaire Belloc, and it became something of a craze amongst them. In 1904 Chesterton went to stay in Yorkshire and met Father John O'Connor of Heckmondwicke (itself the subject of a ballade, and referred to elsewhere in these poems), who immediately became a friend and later served as the model for Father Brown. He tells us that Chesterton wrote ballades 'at the rate of two in a morning under the influence of escape from work and change of air, and he was full of Baring, Bentley and Belloc as well. Ballades had to be exchanged between the club members, and the Envoi had to insult the Prince, the more grossly the better. So it often happened that the Envoi was complete before the ballade was begun, and so it remains in some cases even unto this day. Another rule was that one of the stanzas had to be poetic in flight, with at least one best line.' One of the stray Envois that Father O'Connor quotes is:

> Prince, you are ugly, old, and rather low
> Extremely bald, and very nearly blind:
> The women hate you, and they tell you so,
> But do not let it prey upon your mind.

Chesterton himself sent a telegram to Maurice Baring declining to attend some celebration or other, which ran:

> Prince, Yorkshire holds me now,
> By Yorkshire hams I'm fed.
> I can't assist your row;
> I send ballades instead.

Again, some of the references in these ballades are private and almost incomprehensible even to a close friend like Father O'Connor. Of the lines in 'A Ballade of Reasonable Inquiry',

> When those Raid wires were pawed about and pieced,
> What was that wire whose text has not transpired?,

he notes: 'The Raid in question is the Jameson Raid. For the nearest thing to an explanation, see *The Autobiography of Sir William Butler*.' And see *Father Brown on Chesterton* for further elucidation of these and other matters, in the most delightful manner.

The famous triple portrait of Belloc, Baring and Chesterton by James Gunn, which hangs in London's National Gallery, shows the other two looking on as Chesterton writes in a notebook. It is reportedly the 'Ballade of Devastation' that he was writing out, which he composed with Baring on a day when they sat for the painter and Belloc didn't turn up.

Finally, I should explain that 'The Ballade of a Strange Town' is pieced together from the essay of the same name in which it evolves, in *Tremendous Trifles*. Worth looking out.

VII ... OF WHOM HE WAS EXTREMELY FOND

In this final section of occasional verses, dedications and other such things I have had to be even more selective than elsewhere, for two reasons. The first is that in such a mass of material the level varies hugely; this is not surprising, as many of the inscriptions in books and autograph albums (and there are hundreds of them) were dashed off impromptu to give a moment's pleasure to a friend or acquaintance, and, pleasing as some of them still are, they would be out of place in what purports to be a permanent collection of his best work in this mode. The second is the familiar one of obscurity, even more of a problem when the verse celebrates some private joke or fleeting moment. John Sullivan printed one such piece that he had unearthed, which gave a brief comic history of the Boileau family; by the time that he had explained that the poem was written for a Miss Boileau, who was about to marry E.C. Bentley, Chesterton's boyhood friend, and that her family, of French origin, had been in England since the Huguenot emigration but had remained in contact with the branch of the family that had stayed in France, numbering amongst their common ancestors Etienne Boileau, Grand Provost of Paris in 1250, who *may* have hanged his own son, and so on … well, it seemed an awfully heavy burden to hang upon a very slight poem, and I recoiled from the prospect of page after page of *that*.

What survives can be no more than a brief selection from the mass, but some of the dedications – particularly those addressed to Bentley and to Belloc – are fine poems in their own right, and the others can amuse us almost as much as they must have amused their original recipients. All that one needs to know is that Barbara and Clare (pet-name: Unicorn) were two of the Nicholl children, who lived at nearby Christmas cottage and who became tremendous favourites with the (childless) Chestertons. Barbara also figures in the 'Ballade of a Mackerel Catcher', and a few other poems, while Rhoda (Bastable) was another young chum, whose potential husbands afforded great amusement. The curious will find many more verses of this sort in Maisie Ward's *Return to Chesterton*.

Scattered about the book are various clerihews – those short, irregularly scanned biographical poems so beloved by setters of literary competitions. It has recently been discovered that the original clerihews were written not solely by E.C. Bentley (whose middle name gave them theirs), but by the entire membership of the Junior Debating Club at St Paul's School, of which the young Chesterton was President, with a few additional contributions by Chesterton's father. Their original *Dictionary of Biography*, handwritten by Bentley, illustrated by Chesterton, and published recently in facsimile, gives clues as to who wrote what in the form of pictorial symbols, and it is fascinating to discover that some of the verses later published under Bentley's name were actually written in collaboration with Chesterton, or in a few cases by Chesterton alone. I would not dream of suggesting that this verse-form should be rechristened the gilbert, still less the keith, but it is clear that some of those poems do belong in this book.

Finally, a note on the drawings. Chesterton provided his own delightful illustrations for *Greybeards at Play*, but he illustrated only a few of the other poems included here. I wanted to include these drawings, of course, but it would have created an imbalance, with whole sections of the book left *un*illustrated. After due consultation, it was decided to locate as many as possible of Chesterton's *other* drawings (he was prolific in this respect, too) and see if they could be matched to the verses in a way that would not mis-represent either the pictures or the poems. The publisher's staff have done this with great persistence and considerable ingenuity, and I think with complete success.

MARIE SMITH

I

Greybeards at Play

and other nonsense

I may describe him as a Star
    My best, my only friend
We wore One Hat, smoked One Cigar
  (One standing at Each End)
I always boldly ate the pears
An let him climb the tree
One hope, one toil
            One pair of boots
Joined us eternally —

A DEDICATION
TO E.C.B.

He was, through boyhood's storm and shower,
  My best, my nearest friend;
We wore one hat, smoked one cigar,
  One standing at each end.

We were two hearts with single hope,
  Two faces in one hood;
I knew the secrets of his youth;
  I watched his every mood.

The little things that none but I
  Saw were beyond his wont,
The streaming hair, the tie behind,
  The coat tails worn in front.

I marked the absent-minded scream,
  The little nervous trick
Of rolling in the grate, with eyes
  By friendship's light made quick.

But youth's black storms are gone and past,
  Bare is each aged brow;
And, since with age we're growing bald,
  Let us be babies now.

Learning we knew; but still to-day,
  With spelling-book devotion,
Words of one syllable we seek
  In moments of emotion.

Riches we knew; and well dressed dolls—
  Dolls living—who expressed
No filial thoughts, however much
  You thumped them in the chest.

Old happiness is grey as we,
    And we may still outstrip her;
If we be slippered pantaloons,
    Oh let us hunt the slipper!

The old world glows with colours clear;
    And if, as saith the saint,
The world is but a painted show,
    Oh let us lick the paint!

Far, far behind are morbid hours,
    And lonely hearts that bleed.
Far, far behind us are the days,
    When we were old indeed.

Leave we the child: he is immersed
    With scientists and mystics:
With deep prophetic voice he cries
    Canadian food statistics.

But now I know how few and small,
    The things we crave need be—
Toys and the universe and you—
    A little friend to tea.

Behold the simple sum of things,
    Where, in one splendour spun,
The stars go round the Mulberry Bush,
    The Burning Bush, the Sun.

Now we are old and wise and grey,
    And shaky at the knees;
Now is the true time to delight
    In picture books like these.

Hoary and bent I dance one hour:
    What though I die at morn?
There is a shout among the stars,
    "To-night a child is born."

THE ONENESS OF THE
PHILOSOPHER WITH NATURE

I love to see the little stars
    All dancing to one tune;
I think quite highly of the Sun,
    And kindly of the Moon.

The million forests of the Earth
    Come trooping in to tea.
The great Niagara waterfall
    Is never shy with me.

I am the tiger's confidant,
    And never mention names:
The lion drops the formal 'Sir,'
    And lets me call him James.

Into my ear the blushing Whale
    Stammers his love. I know
Why the Rhinoceros is sad,
    —Ah, child! 'twas long ago.

I am akin to all the Earth
By many a tribal sign:
The aged Pig will often wear
That sad, sweet smile of mine.

My niece, the Barnacle, has got
My piercing eyes of black;
The Elephant has got my nose,
I do not want it back.

I know the strange tale of the Slug;
The Early Sin—the Fall—
The Sleep—the Vision—and the Vow—
The Quest—the Crown—the Call.

And I have loved the Octopus,
Since we were boys together.
I love the Vulture and the Shark:
I even love the weather.

I love to bask in sunny fields,
    And when that hope is vain,
I go and bask in Baker Street,
    All in the pouring rain.

Come snow! where fly, by some strange law,
    Hard snowballs—without noise—
Through streets untenanted, except
    By good unconscious boys.

Come fog! exultant mystery—
    Where, in strange darkness rolled,
The end of my own nose becomes
    A lovely legend old.

Come snow, and hail, and thunderbolts,
    Sleet, fire, and general fuss;
Come to my arms, come all at once—
    Oh photograph me thus!

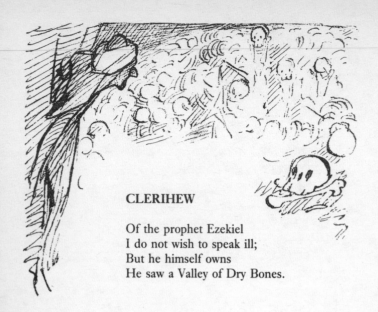

CLERIHEW

Of the prophet Ezekiel
I do not wish to speak ill;
But he himself owns
He saw a Valley of Dry Bones.

WHAT IS A BUSLUS?

The best authorities are vague;
The learned Dr. Bock (of Prague)
Writes "Totally unlike a rat . . ."
I cannot argue much from that.

Pottiger says "Its Knobs are round:
See Beeswax". I have also found
This doubtful note of Dr. Moon,
"Delightful in the afternoon."

Count Posky writes (in joke, I hope)
"Coughs rather like an antelope."
And what can Jupp of Cambridge mean
By saying "Kindness turns it green"?

Some say a Buslus is a bird
And some a science: I have heard

It talked of as a club, a pigeon,
A tool, a fish and a religion.

For many an age, for many an hour,
I've sat and wondered in this tower.
O stars, O seas, O all that is,
I wonder what a Buslus is!

MEDITATION IN RHYME

Of Uncle Humphrey who can sing?
His name can't rhyme with anything,
How much superior is Aunt Harriet
Who rhymes correctly to Iscariot.

OF THE DANGERS ATTENDING
ALTRUISM ON THE HIGH SEAS

Observe these Pirates bold and gay,
    That sail a gory sea:
Notice their bright expression:—
    The handsome one is me.

We plundered ships and harbours,
  We spoiled the Spanish main;
But Nemesis watched over us,
  For it began to rain.

Oh all well-meaning folk take heed!
  Our Captain's fate was sore;
A more well-meaning Pirate,
  Had never dripped with gore.

The rain was pouring long and loud,
  The sea was drear and dim;
A little fish was floating there:
  Our Captain pitied him.

"How sad," he said, and dropped a tear
  Splash on the cabin roof,
"That we are dry, while he is there
  Without a waterproof.

"We'll get him up on board at once;
  For Science teaches me,
He will be wet if he remains
  Much longer in the sea."

They fished him out; the First Mate wept,
  And came with rugs and ale:
The Boatswain brought him one golosh,
  And fixed it on his tail.

But yet he never loved the ship;
  Against the mast he'd lean;
If spoken to, he coughed and smiled,
  And blushed a pallid green.

Though plied with hardbake, beef and beer,
  He showed no wish to sup:
The neatest riddles they could ask,
  He always gave them up.

They seized him and court-martialled him,
  In some excess of spleen,
For lack of social sympathy,
  (Victoria xii. 18).

They gathered every evidence
  That might remove a doubt:
They wrote a postcard in his name,
  And partly scratched it out.

Till, when his guilt was clear as day,
  With all formality
They doomed the traitor to be drowned,
  And threw him in the sea.

The flashing sunset, as he sank,
  Made every scale a gem;
And, turning with a graceful bow,
  He kissed his fin to them.

I am, I think I have remarked,
  Terrifically old,
(The second Ice-age was a farce,
  The first was rather cold.)

A friend of mine, a trilobite
  Had gathered in his youth,
When trilobites *were* trilobites,
  This all-important truth.

We aged ones play solemn parts—
  Sire—guardian—uncle—king.
Affection is the salt of life,
  Kindness a noble thing.

The old alone may comprehend
  A sense in my decree;
But—if you find a fish on land,
  Oh throw it in the sea.

A SONG OF WILD FRUIT

The Pineapple knows nothing
Of the Apple or the Pine,
The Grape-Fruit is a fruit: but not
The God's fruit of the Vine;
And Grape-nuts are not even Nuts
For the Hygienic Hut
Where the nut-crank with the nut-crackers
Is cracking his own nut.

Far in the land of Nonsense Names
These antic fruits were born,
Where men gather grapes of thistles
And the figs grow on the thorn.
And Ananias named the fruit
That Frenchmen call Ananas;
And all the Plantains are a plant,
And . . . No! We have Bananas!

NEVERCOMETRUE

There's a sound of the flutes and the lutes tonight
    In the island of Nevercometrue;
In a fire-lit isle in the seas of the night
    Black with the depth of blue;
And the man that might have been I shall dance
    With the woman that might have been you;
Under the world where a man remembers
    More than he ever knew.

There's a noise of songs in the gongs tonight,
    In the garden of Nevercometrue;
Under the trees of terrible flowers
    That bloom when the moon is blue;
And the man that never was I is wed
    To the woman that never was you—
O nothing nearer than all that is life,
    In Nevercometrue comes true.

ON THE DISASTROUS SPREAD OF
ÆSTHETICISM IN ALL CLASSES

Impetuously I sprang from bed,
  Long before lunch was up,
That I might drain the dizzy dew
  From day's first golden cup.

In swift devouring ecstasy
  Each toil in turn was done;
I had done lying on the lawn
  Three minutes after one.

For me, as Mr. Wordsworth says,
  The duties shine like stars;
I formed my uncle's character,
  Decreasing his cigars.

But could my kind engross me? No!
  Stern Art – what sons escape her?
Soon I was drawing Gladstone's nose
  On scraps of blotting paper.

Then on—to play one-fingered tunes
  Upon my aunt's piano.
In short, I have a headlong soul,
  I much resemble Hanno.

(Forgive the entrance of the not
    Too cogent Carthaginian.
It may have been to make a rhyme;
    I lean to that opinion.)

Then my great work of book research
    Till dusk I took in hand—
The forming of a final, sound
    Opinion on *The Strand*.

But when I quenched the midnight oil,
    And closed *The Referee*,
Whose thirty volumes folio
    I take to bed with me,

I had a rather funny dream,
    Intense, that is, and mystic;
I dreamed that, with one leap and yell,
    The world became artistic.

The Shopmen, when their souls were still,
    Declined to open shops—
And Cooks recorded frames of mind
    In sad and subtle chops.

The stars were weary of routine:
    The trees in the plantation
Were growing every fruit at once,
    In search of a sensation.

The moon went for a moonlight stroll,
    And tried to be a bard,
And gazed enraptured at itself:
    I left it trying hard.

The sea had nothing but a mood
    Of 'vague ironic gloom,'
With which t'explain its presence in
    My upstairs drawing-room.

The sun had read a little book
    That struck him with a notion:
He drowned himself and all his fires
    Deep in the hissing ocean.

Then all was dark, lawless, and lost:
    I heard great devilish wings:
I knew that Art had won, and snapt
    The Covenant of Things.

I cried aloud, and I awoke,
    New labours in my head.
I set my teeth, and manfully
    Began to lie in bed.

Toiling, rejoicing, sorrowing,
    So I my life conduct.
Each morning see some task begun,
    Each evening see it chucked.

But still, in sudden moods of dusk,
    I hear those great weird wings,
Feel vaguely thankful to the vast
    Stupidity of things.

ENVOI

Clear was the night: the moon was young:
    The larkspurs in the plots
Mingled their orange with the gold
    Of the forget-me-nots.

The poppies seemed a silver mist:
    So darkly fell the gloom.
You scarce had guessed yon crimson streaks
    Were buttercups in bloom.

But one thing moved: a little child
    Crashed through the flower and fern:
And all my soul rose up to greet
    The sage of whom I learn.

I looked into his awful eyes:
    I waited his decree:
I made ingenious attempts
    To sit upon his knee.

The babe upraised his wondering eyes,
    And timidly he said,
"A trend towards experiment
    In modern minds is bred.

"I feel the will to roam, to learn
  By test, experience, *nous*,
That fire is hot and ocean deep,
  And wolves carnivorous.

"My brain demands complexity,"
  The lisping cherub cried.
I looked at him, and only said,
  "Go on. The world is wide."

A tear rolled down his pinafore,
  "Yet from my life must pass
The simple love of sun and moon,
  The old games in the grass;

"Now that my back is to my home
  Could these again be found?"
I looked on him, and only said,
  "Go on. The world is round."

CLERIHEWS

Solomon
You can scarcely write less than a column on.
His very song
Was long.

Saul
Was tall.
David cut off the end of his cloak
For a joke.

II

The Rolling English Road

Drinking and travelling songs

THE ENGLISHMAN

St. George he was for England,
And before he killed the dragon
He drank a pint of English ale
Out of an English flagon.
For though he fast right readily
In hair-shirt or in mail,
It isn't safe to give him cakes
Unless you give him ale.

St. George he was for England,
And right gallantly set free
The lady left for dragon's meat
And tied up to a tree;
But since he stood for England
And knew what England means,
Unless you give him bacon
You mustn't give him beans.

St. George he is for England,
And shall wear the shield he wore
When we go out in armour
With the battle-cross before.
But though he is jolly company
And very pleased to dine,
It isn't safe to give him nuts
Unless you give him wine.

Old Noah he had an ostrich farm and
   fowls on the largest scale,
He ate his egg with a ladle in an egg-cup
   big as a pail,
And the soup he took was Elephant Soup
   and the fish he took was Whale,
But they all were small to the cellar he
   took when he set out to sail,
And Noah he often said to his wife when
   he sat down to dine.
"I don't care where the water goes if it
   doesn't get into the wine."

The cataract of the cliff of heaven fell
   blinding off the brink
As if it would wash the stars away as suds
   go down a sink,
The seven heavens came roaring down for
   the throats of hell to drink,
And Noah he cocked his eye and said,
   "It looks like rain, I think,
The water has drowned the Matterhorn
   as deep as a Mendip mine,
But I don't care where the water goes if it
   doesn't get into the wine."

But Noah he sinned, and we have sinned;
    on tipsy feet we trod,
Till a great big black teetotaller was sent
    to us for a rod,
And you can't get wine at a P.S.A., or
    chapel, or Eisteddfod,
For the Curse of Water has come again
    because of the wrath of God,
And water is on the Bishop's board and
    the Higher Thinker's shrine,
But I don't care where the water goes if
    it doesn't get into the wine.

THE SONG AGAINST GROCERS

God made the wicked Grocer
For a mystery and a sign,
That men might shun the awful shops
And go to inns to dine;
Where the bacon's on the rafter
And the wine is in the wood,
And God that made good laughter
Has seen that they are good.

The evil-hearted Grocer
Would call his mother "Ma'am,"
And bow at her and bob at her,
Her aged soul to damn,
And rub his horrid hands and ask
What article was next,
Though *mortis in articulo*
Should be her proper text.

His props are not his children,
But pert lads underpaid,
Who call out "Cash!" and bang about
To work his wicked trade;

He keeps a lady in a cage
Most cruelly all day,
And makes her count and calls her "Miss"
Until she fades away.

The righteous minds of innkeepers
Induce them now and then
To crack a bottle with a friend
Or treat unmoneyed men,
But who hath seen the Grocer
Treat housemaids to his teas
Or crack a bottle of fish-sauce
Or stand a man a cheese?

He sells us sands of Araby
As sugar for cash down;
He sweeps his shop and sells the dust
The purest salt in town,
He crams with cans of poisoned meat
Poor subjects of the King,
And when they die by thousands
Why, he laughs like anything.

The wicked Grocer groces
In spirits and in wine,
Not frankly and in fellowship
As men in inns do dine;
But packed with soap and sardines
And carried off by grooms,
For to be snatched by Duchesses
And drunk in dressing-rooms.

The hell-instructed Grocer
Has a temple made of tin,
And the ruin of good innkeepers
Is loudly urged therein;
But now the sands are running out
From sugar of a sort,
The Grocer trembles; for his time,
Just like his weight, is short.

WHINES FROM THE WOOD

A little sip, a little sip
And then too much.
This is the sort of thing to grip
A duke or duch.
But we who live the life conviv.
We are not such.

We drink and drink and drink and drink,
And then stop short.
"Rum!" says Achates with a wink,
But mine's a port.
The tap's run dry?
Be pleased to try
The other sort.

You don't know how, you don't know how
To broach the bung?
The milkmaid never asked the cow
When I was young,
But simply drank
As from a tank,
The grass among.

Nevertheless, nevertheless,
I am discreet.
Despite the chill of bitterness,
True love is sweet.
Though hearts may ache,
A prime rump steak
Is good to eat.

Despite the smart, despite the smart,
The Lord has had
A corner for me in his heart—
The dear old lad!
And God's my friend,
And that's the end,
And aren't you glad.

A CIDER SONG

TO J.S.M.

Extract from a Romance which is not yet
written and probably never will be.

The wine they drink in Paradise
They make in Haute Lorraine;
God brought it burning from the sod
To be a sign and signal rod
That they that drink the blood of God
Shall never thirst again.

The wine they praise in Paradise
They make in Ponterey,
The purple wine of Paradise,
But we have better at the price;
It's wine they praise in Paradise,
It's cider that they pray.

The wine they want in Paradise
They find in Plodder's End,
The apple wine of Hereford,
Of Hafod Hill, and Hereford,
Where woods went down to Hereford,
And there I had a friend.

The soft feet of the blessed go
In the soft western vales,
The road the silent saints accord,
The road from heaven to Hereford,
Where the apple wood of Hereford
Goes all the way to Wales.

THE ROLLING ENGLISH ROAD

Before the Roman came to Rye or out to
    Severn strode,
The rolling English drunkard made the
    rolling English road.

A reeling road, a rolling road, that
    rambles round the shire,
And after him the parson ran, the sexton
    and the squire;
A merry road, a mazy road, and such as
    we did tread
The night we went to Birmingham by
    way of Beachy Head.

I knew no harm of Bonaparte and plenty
    of the Squire,
And for to fight the Frenchman I did not
    much desire;
But I did bash their baggonets because
    they came arrayed
To straighten out the crooked road an
    English drunkard made,
Where you and I went down the lane
    with ale-mugs in our hands,
The night we went to Glastonbury by
    way of Goodwin Sands.

His sins they were forgiven him; or why
  do flowers run
Behind him; and the hedges all
  strengthening in the sun?
The wild thing went from left to right
  and knew not which was which,
But the wild rose was above him when
  they found him in the ditch.
God pardon us, nor harden us; we did
  not see so clear
The night we went to Bannockburn by
  way of Brighton Pier.

My friends, we will not go again or ape
  an ancient rage,
Or stretch the folly of our youth to be
  the shame of age,
But walk with clearer eyes and ears this
  path that wandereth,
And see undrugged in evening light the
  decent inn of death;
For there is good news yet to hear and
  fine things to be seen,
Before we go to Paradise by way of
  Kensal Green.

THE SONG OF QUOODLE[1]

They haven't got no noses,
The fallen sons of Eve;
Even the smell of roses
Is not what they supposes;
But more than mind discloses
And more than men believe.

They haven't got no noses,
They cannot even tell

[1] Quoodle is a dog.

When door and darkness closes
The park a Jew encloses,
Where even the Law of Moses
Will let you steal a smell.

The brilliant smell of water,
The brave smell of a stone,
The smell of dew and thunder,
The old bones buried under,
Are things in which they blunder
And err, if left alone.

The wind from winter forests,
The scent of scentless flowers,
The breath of brides' adorning,
The smell of snare and warning,
The smell of Sunday morning
God gave to us for ours.

* * *

And Quoodle here discloses
All things that Quoodle can.
They haven't got no noses,
They haven't got no noses,
And goodness only knowses
The Noselessness of Man.

THE GOOD RICH MAN

Mr. Mandragon, the Millionaire, he wouldn't have wine or wife,
He couldn't endure complexity; he lived the simple life.
He ordered his lunch by megaphone in manly, simple tones,
And used all his motors for canvassing voters, and twenty telephones;
Besides a dandy little machine,
Cunning and neat as ever was seen
With a hundred pulleys and cranks between,
Made of metal and kept quite clean,
To hoist him out of his healthful bed on every day of his life,
And wash him and brush him, and shave him and dress him to live the
   Simple Life.

Mr. Mandragon was most refined and quietly, neatly dressed,
Say all the American newspapers that know refinement best;
Neat and quiet the hair and hat, and the coat quiet and neat.
A trouser worn upon either leg, while boots adorn the feet;
And not, as any one might expect,
A Tiger Skin, all striped and flecked,
And a Peacock Hat with the tail erect,
A scarlet tunic with sunflowers decked,
—That might have had a more marked effect,
And pleased the pride of a weaker man that yearned for wine or wife;
But fame and the flagon, for Mr. Mandragon obscured the Simple
 Life.

Mr. Mandragon the Millionaire, I am happy to say, is dead;
He enjoyed a quiet funeral in a crematorium shed,
And he lies there fluffy and soft and grey, and certainly quite refined,
When he might have rotted to flowers and fruit with Adam and all
 mankind,
Or been eaten by wolves athirst for blood,
Or burnt on a big tall pyre of wood,
In a towering flame, as a heathen should,
Or even sat with us here at food,
Merrily taking twopenny ale and cheese with a pocket-knife;
But these were luxuries not for him who went for the Simple Life.

SONGS FOR BANK CLERKS[1]

I

Up my lads, and lift the ledgers, sleep and ease are o'er.
  Hear the Stars of Morning shouting: "Two and Two
  are Four."
Though the creeds and realms are reeling, though the
  sophists roar,
Though we weep and pawn our watches, Two and Two
  are Four.

II

There's a run upon the Bank—
  Stand away!
For the Manager's a crank and the Secretary drank, and
  the Upper Tooting Bank
    Turns to bay!

Stand close: there is a run
  On the Bank.
Of our ship, our royal one, let the ringing legend run,
  that she fired with every gun
    Ere she sank.

POST OFFICE HYMN (SPECIMEN VERSE)

O'er London our letters are shaken like snow,
Our wires o'er the world like the thunderbolts go.
The news that may marry a maiden in Sark,
Or kill an old lady in Finsbury Park.

  Chorus (with a swing of joy and energy):

Or kill an old lady in Finsbury Park.

---

[1] If reapers sing while reaping, why should not auditors sing while auditing and bankers while banking? –G.K.C

THE ROAD TO ROUNDABOUT

Some say that Guy of Warwick,
The man that killed the Cow
And brake the mighty Boar alive
Beyond the Bridge at Slough;
Went up against a Loathly Worm
That wasted all the Downs,
And so the roads they twist and squirm
(If I may be allowed the term)
From the writhing of the stricken Worm
That died in seven towns.
   I see no scientific proof
   That this idea is sound,
   And I should say they wound about
   To find the town of Roundabout,
   The merry town of Roundabout,
   That makes the world go round.

Some say that Robin Goodfellow,
Whose lantern lights the meads
(To steal a phrase Sir Walter Scott
In heaven no longer needs),
Such dance around the trysting-place
The moonstruck lover leads;
Which superstition I should scout
There is more faith in honest doubt
(As Tennyson has pointed out)
Than in those nasty creeds.
   But peace and righteousness (St. John)
   In Roundabout can kiss,
   And since that's all that's found about
   The pleasant town of Roundabout,
   The roads they simply bound about
   To find out where it is.

Some say that when Sir Lancelot
Went forth to find the Grail,
Grey Merlin wrinkled up the roads
For hope that he should fail;
All roads led back to Lyonesse

And Camelot in the Vale,
I cannot yield assent to this
Extravagant hypothesis,
The plain, shrewd Briton will dismiss
Such rumours (*Daily Mail*).
    But in the streets of Roundabout
    Are no such factions found,
    Or theories to expound about,
    Or roll upon the ground about,
    In the happy town of Roundabout,
    That makes the world go round.

THE SONG AGAINST SONGS

The song of the sorrow of Melisande is a weary song and a dreary
    song,
The glory of Mariana's grange had got into great decay,
The song of the Raven Never More has never been called a cheery
    song,
And the brightest things in Baudelaire are anything else but gay.

But who will write us a riding song
Or a hunting song or a drinking song,
Fit for them that arose and rode
When day and the wine were red?
But bring me a quart of claret out,
And I will write you a clinking song,
A song of war and a song of wine
And a song to wake the dead.

The song of the fury of Fragolette is a florid song and a torrid song,
The song of the sorrow of Tara is sung to a harp unstrung,
The song of the cheerful Shropshire Lad I consider a perfectly
    horrid song,
And the song of the happy Futurist is a song that can't be sung.

But who will write us a riding song
Or a fighting song or a drinking song,
Fit for the fathers of you and me,
That know how to think and thrive?

But the song of Beauty and Art and Love
Is simply an utterly stinking song,
To double you up and drag you down
And damn your soul alive.

THE SONG OF THE STRANGE ASCETIC

If I had been a Heathen,
  I'd have praised the purple vine,
My slaves should dig the vineyards,
  And I would drink the wine.
But Higgins is a Heathen,
  And his slaves grow lean and grey,
That he may drink some tepid milk
  Exactly twice a day.

If I had been a Heathen,
  I'd have crowned Neœra's curls,
And filled my life with love affairs,
  My house with dancing girls;
But Higgins is a Heathen,
  And to lecture rooms is forced,
Where his aunts, who are not married,
  Demand to be divorced.

If I had been a Heathen,
  I'd have sent my armies forth,
And dragged behind my chariots
  The Chieftains of the North.
But Higgins is a Heathen,
  And he drives the dreary quill,
To lend the poor that funny cash
  That makes them poorer still.

If I had been a Heathen,
  I'd have piled my pyre on high,
And in a great red whirlwind
  Gone roaring to the sky;

But Higgins is a Heathen,
  And a richer man than I:
And they put him in an oven,
  Just as if he were a pie.

Now who that runs can read it,
  The riddle that I write,
Of why this poor old sinner,
  Should sin without delight—?
But I, I cannot read it
  (Although I run and run),
Of them that do not have the faith,
  And will not have the fun.

THE SONG OF RIGHT AND WRONG

Feast on wine or fast on water,
And your honour shall stand sure,
God Almighty's son and daughter
He the valiant, she the pure;
If an angel out of heaven
Brings you other things to drink.
Thank him for his kind attentions,
Go and pour them down the sink.

Tea is like the East he grows in,
A great yellow Mandarin
With urbanity of manner
And unconsciousness of sin;

All the women, like a harem,
At his pig-tail troop along;
And, like all the East he grows in,
He is Poison when he's strong.

Tea, although an Oriental,
Is a gentleman at least;
Cocoa is a cad and coward,
Cocoa is a vulgar beast,
Cocoa is a dull, disloyal,
Lying, crawling cad and clown,
And may very well be grateful
To the fool that takes him down.

As for all the windy waters,
They were rained like tempests down
When good drink had been dishonoured
By the tipplers of the town:
When red wine had brought red ruin
And the death-dance of our times,
Heaven sent us Soda Water
As a torment for our crimes.

THE GOOD GROCER
(AN APOLOGY)

Babes, when I too was young and always right
And tangled in that not unrighteous fight
Beneath the Wooden Flag, the Painted Sign,
We poured our blood—or anyhow our wine—
For feast of all our fathers, and liberties;
Not having Charity before my eyes
I cursed a Grocer . . . saying that he, by fault,
Put sand in sugar and no salt in salt,
Trapped men with stinking fish that leapt from tins;
And rising to the toppling top of sins
Discouraged Pubs and spoilt the English Inns.

The Heavens, I learn as still I linger and live,
Punish more generously than men forgive,

No grinning Grocer slew me with a sweet,
I writhed across no tins of poisoned meat;
Only . . . where far in the warm western shires
Steep stooping woods are dipped in sunset fires
The children told me that, aloof, alone,
Dwelt the Good Grocer whom I had not known.

Ah, not forgotten, the children that I knew,
Not if they died—not even if they grew—
How their locks flamed and limbs like arrows sped
And faces shone with the wild news they said:
The Fairy Grocer—his were magic sales,
His books might have been filled with fairy tales;
He might have tipped sardines back in the sea,
Given all his goods away with a pound of tea;
Sanding no sugar, on the other hand,
Have spread his sugar o'er the shores for sand:
Till children came unto those yellow sands
And there took hands—and handfuls in their hands
And mouthfuls in their mouths; stuffed more and more
Till they had made erosion of the shore,
Bit bays and inlets out of all the coast
Like giant bites out of titanic toast.

To you dear children of old days, I send
This apologia to your carly friend,
You know, though I said salt was dust in mirth,
Our dust can still be salt, and salt of the earth;
A Wizard is an easier thing to be
Than being a Good Grocer, as is he.

III

The Worshipper's Half-Holiday

Parodies and burlesques

THE NEW OMAR

A book of verses underneath the bough,
   Provided that the verses do not scan,
A loaf of bread, a jug of wine and Thou,
   Short-haired, all angles, looking like a man.

But let the wine be unfermented, pale,
   Of chemicals compounded, God knows how—
This were indeed the Prophet's Paradise,
   O Paradise were Wilderness enow.

VARIATIONS OF AN AIR:
COMPOSED ON HAVING TO APPEAR IN A PAGEANT AS OLD KING COLE

Old King Cole was a merry old soul,
And a merry old soul was he;
He called for his pipe,
He called for his bowl,
And he called for his fiddlers three.

After Lord Tennyson

Cole, that unwearied prince of Colchester,
Growing more gay with age and with long days

Deeper in laughter and desire of life,
As that Virginian climber on our walls
Flames scarlet with the fading of the year;
Called for his wassail and that other weed
Virginian also, from the western woods
Where English Raleigh checked the boast of Spain,
And lighting joy with joy, and piling up
Pleasure as crown for pleasure, bade men bring
Those three, the minstrels whose emblazoned coats
Shone with the oyster-shells of Colchester;
And these three played, and playing grew more fain
Of mirth and music; till the heathen came,
And the King slept beside the northern sea.

After W. B. Yeats

Of an old King in a story
    From the grey sea-folk I have heard,
Whose heart was no more broken
    Than the wings of a bird.

As soon as the moon was silver
    And the thin stars began,
He took his pipe and his tankard,
    Like an old peasant man.

And three tall shadows were with him
    And came at his command;
And played before him for ever
    The fiddles of fairyland.

And he died in the young summer
    Of the world's desire;
Before our hearts were broken
    Like sticks in a fire.

After Robert Browning

Who smoke-snorts toasts o' My Lady Nicotine,
Kicks stuffing out of Pussyfoot, bids his trio
Stick up their Stradivarii (that's the plural)
Or near enough, my fatheads; *nimium*
Vicina Cremonæ; that's a bit too near).
Is there some stockfish fails to understand?
Catch hold o' the notion, bellow and blurt back
    "Cole"?
Must I bawl lessons from a horn-book, howl,
Cat-call the cat-gut "fiddles"? Fiddlesticks!

After Walt Whitman

Me clairvoyant,
Me conscious of you, old camarado,
Needing no telescope, lorgnette, field-glass, opera-glass,
    myopic pince-nez,
Me piercing two thousand years with eye naked and not ashamed;
The crown cannot hide you from me;
Musty old feudal-heraldic trappings cannot hide you from me,
I perceive that you drink.
(I am drinking with you. I am as drunk as you are.)
I see you are inhaling tobacco, puffing, smoking, spitting
(I do not object to your spitting),
You prophetic of American largeness,
You anticipating the broad masculine manners of these States;
I see in you also there are movements, tremors, tears, desire for the
    melodious,
I salute your three violinists, endlessly making vibrations,
Rigid, relentless, capable of going on for ever;
They play my accompaniment; but I shall take no notice of any
    accompaniment;
I myself am a complete orchestra.
So long.

After Swinburne

In the time of old sin without sadness
    And golden with wastage of gold

Like the gods that grow old in their gladness
    Was the king that was glad, growing old;
And with sound of loud lyres from his palace
    The voice of his oracles spoke,
And the lips that were red from his chalice
    Were splendid with smoke.
When the weed was as flame for a token
    And the wine was as blood for a sign;
And upheld in his hands and unbroken
    The fountains of fire and of wine.
And a song without speech, without singer,
    Stung the soul of a thousand in three
As the flesh of the earth has to sting her,
    The soul of the sea.

from THE GOLDEN TREASURY REGILDED; OR, THE CLASSICS MADE COCKNEY

Therefore, ye gas-pipes, ye asbestos stoves,
Forbode not any severing of our loves.
I have relinquished but your earthly sight,
To hold you dear in a more distant way.
I'll love the 'buses lumbering through the wet,
Even more than when I lightly tripped as they.
The grimy colour of the London clay
Is lovely yet . . .

LINES BY THE LATE LORD TENNYSON

(On Miss Spencer being transferred with
her typewriter from the study to the dining room)

Of old sat Freda on the heights
The letters strewn about her feet.
She watched from far the local sights,
She saw the neighbours meet.

She murmured much of fools and worms,
Self-censured in her Christian mind,
And fragments of abusive terms
Came rolling on the wind.

Yet came she down when gongs had pealed
In friendship to our feasting place,
Removed her goggles and revealed
The fulness of her face.

ANSWERS TO THE POETS

THE SKYLARK REPLIES TO WORDSWORTH
(As it might have appeared to Byron)

Ephemeral minstrel, staring at the sky,
    Dost thou despise the earth where wrongs abound,
Or, eyeing me, hast thou the other eye
    Still on the Court, with pay-day coming round,
That pension that could bring thee down at will
Those rebel wings composed, that protest still?

Past the last trace of meaning and beyond
    Mount, daring babbler, that pay-prompted strain
'Twixt thee and Kings a never-failing bond
    Swells not the less their carnage o'er the plain.
Type of the wise, who drill but never fight,
True to the kindred points of Might and Right.

THE SEA REPLIES TO BYRON
(As it might have appeared to Wordsworth)

Stroll on, thou dark not deep "blue" dandy, stroll,
    Ten thousand duns call after thee in vain.
'Thy tailor's marked with ruin; his control
    Stops with my shore; beyond he doth retain
No shadow of a chance of what's his own,
But sinks above his bills with bubbling groan,
"Absconded; gone abroad; address unknown."

Thy songs are speeches, void of all save Thee,
    Childe Harold, Lara, Manfred, what care I?
My water washed them down—you got it free,
    And many a wine-cup since when you were dry,
Till nature blows the man-hater sky-high,
Howling against his gods in stark D.T.,
And dashes him against the Truth. There let him *lie*.

THE FAT WHITE WOMAN SPEAKS

Why do you rush through the field in trains,
Guessing so much and so much.
Why do you flash through the flowery meads,
Fat-head poet that nobody reads;
And why do you know such a frightful lot
About people in gloves as such?
And how the devil can you be sure,
Guessing so much and so much,
How do you know but what someone who loves
Always to see me in nice white gloves
At the end of the field you are rushing by,
Is waiting for his Old Dutch?

LUCASTA REPLIES TO LOVELACE

Tell me not, friend, you are unkind,
   If ink and books laid by,
You turn up in a uniform
   Looking all smart and spry.

I thought your ink one horrid smudge,
   Your books one pile of trash,
And with less fear of smear embrace
   A sword, a belt, a sash.

Yet this inconstancy forgive,
   Though gold lace I adore,
I could not love the lace so much
   Loved I not Lovelace more.

BY A CAPTAIN, OR PERHAPS A COLONEL, OR POSSIBLY A KNIGHT-AT-ARMS

Poet or pamphleteer, or what you please,
Who chance behind this space of wall to dwell,
Upon my soul I cannot very well
Correct my fire for arguments like these,
The great Emathian conquerer be blowed!
I have not got a spear or you a bower.
London is packed with poets; temple and tower
Swarm with them; where the devil should we be
Storming a town, if the repeated plea
Of Puritanic poets had the power
To stop a piece of ordnance with an ode?

FROM THE SPANISH CLOISTER

Grrrr—what's that? A dog? A poet?
   Uttering his damnations thus—
If hate killed things, Brother Browning,
   God's Word, would not hate kill us?

If we ever meet together,
   Salve tibi! I might hear

How you know poor monks are really
   So much worse than they appear.

There's a great text in Corinthians
   Hinting that our faith entails
Something else, that never faileth,
   Yet in you, perhaps, it fails.

But if *plena gratia* chokes you,
   You at least can teach us how
To converse in wordless noises,
   Hy, zi; hullo!—Grrrr—Bow-wow!

DOLORES REPLIES TO SWINBURNE

Cold passions, and perfectly cruel,
   Long odes that go on for an hour,
With a most economical jewel
   And a quite metaphorical flower.
I implore you to stop it and stow it,
   I adjure you, relent and refrain,
Oh, pagan Priapean poet,
       You give me a pain.

I am sorry, old dear, if I hurt you,
   No doubt it is all very nice
With the lilies and languors of virtue
   And the raptures and roses of vice.
But the notion impels me to anger,
   That vice is all rapture for me,
And if you think virtue is languor
       Just try it and see.

We shall know when the critics discover
   If your poems were shallow or deep;
Who read you from cover to cover,
   Will know if they sleep not or sleep.
But you say I've endured through the ages
   (Which is rude) as Our Lady of Pain,
You have said it for several pages,
       So say it again.

LADY CLARA VERE DE VERE REPLIES TO
MR. ALFRED TENNYSON

Alfred, Alfred Tennyson,
  So you've come up to Town as well!
We saw you in the Park to-day,
  And scarcely knew you, such a swell.
You don't desire the *Daily Wire*
  Should print your name with father's guests;
We'd ask you here to meet the Prince,
  But you have loftier interests.

Listen, Alfred Tennyson,
  It's not the best of taste, you know,
To blame me for what I myself
  Was forced to suffer, years ago.
Your Muse forgets the racing debts
  I paid three times before the day
When Laurence in the lime-walk flung
  His panic-stricken life away.

Alfred, Alfred Tennyson,
  Till she can see me clapped in goal
His mother's pledged my name; and you
  Sit still and let the creature rail.
The jury found his mind unsound,
  And hers is balanced none too well;
But in what dark unstable realms
  Your generous soul prefers to dwell!

Really, Alfred Tennyson,
   You move a bit behind the times.
There's not an orphan, girl or boy,
   That can't by heart repeat your rhymes.
For girls indeed are taught to read
   While beggars at the castle gate
Don't find much use for simple faith.
   Oh, Alfred, do get up to date!

TO A MODERN POET

      Well,
      What
      about it?

am sorry
   if you have
      a green pain
gnawing your brain away.
      I suppose
quite a lot of it is
      gnawed away
         by this time.

I did not give you
      a green pain
      or even
      a grey powder.
It is rather you, so winged, so vortical,
   Who give me a pain.
When I have a pain
      I never notice
         the colour.

But I am very unobservant.
      I cannot say
I ever noticed that the pillar-box
   was like a baby
      skinned alive and screaming.
      I have not
      a Poet's

                    Eye
              which can see Beauty
                  everywhere.

        Now you mention it,
              Of course, the sky
                 is like a large mouth
                     shown to a dentist,
        and I never noticed
            a little thing
                 like that.

        But I can't help wishing
              You got more fun out of it;
              you seem to have taken
                  quite a dislike
                      to things
        They seem to make you jump
        And double up unexpectedly—

        And when you write
              like other poets,
                  on subjects
        not entirely
                  novel,
              such as, for instance,
                  the Sea,
        it is mostly about
              Sea-sickness.
        As you say—
        It is the New Movement,
              The Emetic Ecstacy.

POST-RECESSIONAL

God of your fathers, known of old,
     For patience with man's swaggering line,
He did not answer you when told
     About you and your palm and pine,
Though you deployed your far-flung host
And boasted that you did not boast.

Though drunk with sight of power and blind,
   Even as you bowed your head in awe,
You kicked up both your heels behind
   At lesser breeds without the law;
Lest they forget, lest they forget,
That yours was the exclusive set.

We fancied heaven preferring much,
   Your rowdiest song, your slangiest sentence,
Your honest banjo banged, to such
   Very recessional repentance;
Now if your native land be dear,
Whisper (or shout) and we shall hear.

Cut down, our navies melt away.
   From ode and war-song fades the fire,
We are a jolly sight to-day
   Too near to Sidon and to Tyre
To make it sound so very nice
To offer ancient sacrifice.

Rise up and bid the trumpets blow
   When it is gallant to be gay,
Tell the wide world it shall not know
   Our face until we turn to bay.
Bless you, you shall be blameless yet,
For God forgives and men forget.

SONNET TO A STILTON CHEESE

Stilton, thou shouldst be living at this hour.
And so thou art. Nor losest grace thereby;
England has need of thee, and so have I—
She is a Fen. Far as the eye can scour,
League after grassy league from Lincoln tower
To Stilton in the fields, she is a Fen.
Yet this high cheese, by vhoice of fenland men,
Like a tall green volcano rose in power.

Plain living and long drinking are no more,
And pure religion, reading *Household Words*,
And sturdy manhood, sitting still all day,
Shrink, like this cheese that crumbles to its core;
While my digestion, like the House of Lords,
The heaviest burdens on herself doth lay.

ALL THROUGH THE NIGHT

(The effect of these lines depends entirely on
their being sung very slowly indeed to the beautiful
Welsh air.)

Jazz is jerking, jazzers recling,
    All through the night!
Raucous saxophones are pealing
    All through the night.
Din like all damnation dealing—
Yelling, banging, howling, squealing,
Suit this air when played with feeling
    All through the night.

Noise that keeps the night-clubs going
    All through the night.
Fizz and cocktails always flowing
    All through the night.
Showy women not worth showing;
Men well-known and not worth knowing—
Loudly their own trumpets blowing
    All through the night.

Naught can stay the mad gyrations
   All through the night.
Or the latest chic sensations
   All through the night.
Save alarming indications
That the local police stations,
Also stretch their operations—
   All through the night.

Woeful poet, sit not weeping
   All through the night.
Peace a wiser world is steeping
   All through the night.
They that have our lives in keeping:
Digging, planting, ploughing, reaping,
Still retain a taste for sleeping—
   All through the night.

SCHOOL
ENGLISH COMPOSITION

Exercise CCXXII. B: The "TOMATO" in Prose and Prosody.

No subject has so deeply agitated modern life, or presented so profound a problem to the modern conscience, as the matter of the different pronunciations of the word "tomato", and all lesser matters of morals, manners, religion and civilization may well be set aside, and their barren quarrels suspended, while this vital matter is decided in the serious manner it demands.

Already a divergence of pronunciation on this point has divided the two great Anglo-Saxon communities, on whose friendship depends the peace of the world, our American cousins preferring, for reasons best known to themselves, to prounce "tomato" as if it were meant to rhyme to "potato." Thus, in the little known companion poem to "The Village Blacksmith" entitled "The Village Greengrocer", the poet Longfellow observes with a simplicity that is his alone

> If you meet the Village Maiden
> Pause: and give her a tomato:
> Or if shyly she refuse it.
> Offer her a large potato.

But this pronunciation was no provincialism of the rustic and the innocent. In the famous passage in "The Raven", Edgar Allen Poe himself writes:

With a heart as cold as Cato's, or the pallid bust of Plato's,
That I keep with canned tomatoes just above my chamber door.

On the other hand the typical outburst of Walt Whitman concerning "Tomatoes: tomatoes everywhere, raw, red, utterly uneatable: me myself also as raw and red as any tomato," does not, with all its quiet beauty, throw any light on the elocutionary question.

But a graver question has arisen touching the accentuation of the word. Even our Anglo-Saxon cousins apparently manage to agree with us in accenting the penultimate syllable. There has, however, appeared in the West Country, a poetical group, a nest of singing-birds, described by hostile critics as a nest of Roman Catholics, who openly accent the first syllable to the word, turning it into a dactyl, and producing a sound resembling that of "tommy-toes."

Authorities are not easy to adduce. Shakespeare has only one doubtful reference to tomatoes, on which the commentators differ: Duffins reading "comatose" and Boxsheim "come at once." Milton's description of the light lunch given by Eve to Adam,

Tomatoes tolerant and cucumber mild,

is not, to anyone familiar with Miltonic variations, final touching his view of tomatoes, though decisive enough of his very Miltonic emphasis on cucumbers. The eighteenth century is almost silent. The tomato is too wild and fantastic an object to grow in the trim rose-garden of Pope or even of Cowper. Burns indeed has the line:

> Wisht grumly claucht tomato tizzy

but it is not easy to infer the sound of one word in a line, while we cannot reproduce the sound of any of the others.

There follows a gap: Byron, with his hasty arrogance, ignored the tomato: its presence escaped the drugged abstraction of Coleridge. Curiously enough, a tomato is almost the only object in the universe to which Shelley does not compare the Cloud or the Skylark. And it adds a darker shade to the tragedy of the early death of Keats to reflect that, had he lived and his powers expanded, he would doubtless have given his best work to the rich and glowing topic of tomatoes. With the Victorians the tomato reappears—like the pomegranate. Tennyson's stress is as usual traditional,

> The ripe tomato grows from green to red
> As grows from green to red the dusk of day.

But Swinburne is for the revolutionary prosody,

> When red were the apples of Venus
> And bitter with poisonous mirth
> When tomatoes panted between us,
> Red tomatoes bursting at birth.

Mr. W.B. Yeats appears to follow his first masters, the Pre-Raphaelite poets, in this as in some other things; but his later poetic license leaves the point doubtful.

> I went into Kidnoggin Wood
> With a dried laughter in my mind:
> I tore seven tomatoes with my teeth
> For laughter never can be kind.

Here it seems probable that the new dactylic scansion is employed. The rather irregular verse of Miss Edith Sitwell,

> The sky bulges through the skylight like a blue tomato,

throws no light on what accent she gives to the word, or indeed on what meaning she attaches to it.

NOTE: There is a poem by Browning, which the Browning Society believes to be about a tomato: but as the word is not used and the poem is entitled "Ben-Hafiz Self-Examines," the question of pronunciation does not arise.

IV
Bob-up-and-Down

More nonsense

TRIOLET

I wish I were a jelly fish
That cannot fall downstairs:
Of all the things I wish to wish
I wish I were a jelly fish
That hasn't any cares,
And doesn't even have to wish
'I wish I were a jelly fish
That cannot fall downstairs.'

HENRY CHARD

I knew a youth named Henry Chard,
   Whose grandpa was deceased;
His grandma lived by selling lard,
His mother worked extremely hard,
His uncle was a railway guard,
   His father was a beast.

When Christmas came with green and red,
   And everything it means,
His grandpa went on being dead,
His grandma gave him rolls of thread,
His uncle, soldiers made of lead,
His mother even gave him bread,
   His father gave him beans.

A certain day, when Henry Chard
  Was standing on his head,
And turning cartwheels very hard,
The King came by with all his Guard,
With officers all plumed and starred,
And said, "I wish, oh Master Chard,
  I could do that instead."

He tried in vain: then, with a sigh,
  Our Henry he did choose
And made him Duke and C.S.I.
And Z.P.C. and K.X.Y.,
And he was everything that's high,
Till he at last was mentioned by
  The current "Daily News".

When Henry Chard heard this, his gay
  Indifference was shocking;
He said, "I won't be A.Q.K.,
Or X.Y.L., or P.D.A.
Your friends are Dukes, I guess, and they
Seem to be anything but gay,
And all I want on Christmas Day
  Is something in my stocking."

The King he swore a mighty vow,
  And did not seek to hide it:
"By Heaven and this Imperial brow,
There's something in your stocking now
That Heaven has put there, Heaven knows how,
  Though you have never spied it:
A wonderful thing with ears and eyes,
And cartwheels turned, and wonderful cries.
Oh! the self is sad and the soul is gone,
For all the kings that the sun shone on;
But well for you, when all is done,
If you can pull your stocking on
  And find yourself inside it."

CLERIHEW

Though Irish, Lawrence Sterne
Was no mere kerne
If he had been a kerne, he
Couldn't have written "A Sentimental Journey."

THE LITERAL LAND

*The heroine who is a Pearl-fisher dwelling on an islet off Fairyland is fished
up on board. She explains to the people on the yacht the law of Fairyland,
that everything is realised which anyone mentions or desires.*

Through secret seas of blue and gold and skies of blood and fire
We sail with leaping canvas to the Land of Heart's Desire.
No wonder that its skies are queer, all red and green and grey
When the people there are wishing different weathers all the day.

But O my friends, of naughty names and similes beware;
When Uncle Brown is rude at tea don't call him "an old bear"
For you'll be even more disturbed when in a flash you see
A grizzly Bear as big as a house sit bolt upright to tea.

If you should call your children "pigs" because they bite their nails
The incautious word will fill the room with squeaks and curly tails.
A man once said "the lion's share" with metaphoric pride;
He was eaten by his metaphor—which is not dignified.

When merry friends around your board incline to sing and spout
Don't talk about your quarters as the place where you "hang out"
For it is really awkward from Society to swing—
And find yourself outside the window, flapping on a string.

But once my eyes beheld a sight that baffled blood and breath,
To paint it were a madman's dream, to dream of it were death.
The screaming farmers reeled afar, the fowls of heaven fled off
For in the centre stood the horse who really ate his head off.

Through secret seas of green and gold and skies of blood and fire
We sail with leaping canvas to the Land of Heart's Desire.
We're near it now: I've warned you—I've told you all I've seen
If we make any muddles now we must be jolly green

(screams) Ah!

(The whole group has gone green in a strong emerald light thrown on the stage. They all rise in tumult. The ship has crossed the boundary.)

CLERIHEWS

Dean Colet
Would have hated Smollett.
Whether they ever actually met
I really forget.

"Currer Bell"
Was all very well;
I like her rather,
But as for her father—!

J.H. Spurgeon
Was a queer old sturgeon.
His opponents he would tackle
In a tabernacle.

THE SONGS OF THE MOONCALF

I

Oh, my limbs are very feeble,
My head is very big,
My ears are round, O do not, pray
Mistake me for a pig.

II

This Calf was the Mooncalf, the Cow was the Moon,
She died from effects of a popular tune,
And now in her glory she shines in the sky;
Oh, never had Calf such a mother as I.

I forget all the creatures that taunt and despise,
When through the dark night-mists my mother doth rise,
She is tender and kind and she shines the night long
On her lunatic child as he sings her his song.
I was dropped on the dim earth to wander alone,
And save this pale monster no child she hath known
Without like on the earth, without sister or brother
I sit here and sing to my mystical mother.

On thy poor offspring thy pale beams be given,
Turning the dull moor to white halls of heaven,
And in my songs, O Cow, from your memory slide off
The painful effects of the tune that you died of.
We sit here alone, but a joy to each other,
The light to the child and the songs to the mother.

A WISH

I wish I were a Girl Guide,
And looked so bright and neat
And made my young subordinates
Salute me in the street.
But none have ever called me neat
And few have thought me bright
And the young who see me are amused
And double up at sight.

I wish I were a Girl Guide,
And wore so large a hat
Curled up abruptly at the side
With a nice cockade like that.
My hat is large but shabby
And without that cock or curl
Few would mistake me for a guide
Or even for a girl.

GIRL GUIDES

When Cleopatra was made a Guide,
She let her militant duties slide,
And when her prattle had lost the battle
Tactfully tickled a snake and died.

When Boadicea was made a Guide,
Her visage the vividest blue was dyed;
So the coat was made of a similar shade
And she travelled on wheels with the spokes outside.

When Lady Godiva was made a Guide,
The uniform had to be simplified,
But the rates were high, and she was not shy,
And they say it was only the horse that shied.

When Bloody Mary was made a Guide,
She told the people that when she died
Topographical notes on her views and her votes
If they took her to bits would be found inside.

When Queen Victoria was made a Guide,
She never excelled on the giant stride,
Or won a place in the obstacle race,
And historians doubt if she even tried.

When Messalina was made a Guide . . .
. . . But the trouble is that the form I've tried,
Though far from clever, might last for ever,
With hundreds and hundreds of names beside.

SONG OF THE CONSPIRATORS

What do you know about people who go about
Raiding a village like tramps?
Storming the shops for improbable objects,
Buying superfluous stamps:
Shouting for anything, mud or mixed pickles,
Stroking a nigerous cat:
What do you know of the way of the Nicholls?
What do you know about that?

What do you know about people who blow about
Lyme, and along the parade,
Where in the solemn sarcophagous shelter
In its funereal shade
Poor old G.K. (who is perfectly chronic)
Talks through his Horrible Hat—
Under the gloom of the columns Ionic
What do you know about that?

What do you know about what is the Show about
Destined to knock you all flat—
What do you know of ......[1]
What do you know about that?

CLERIHEWS

The Spanish people think Cervantes
Equal to half a dozen Dantes;
An opinion resented most bitterly
By the people of Italy.

Sir Richard Steele
Lived on orange peel;
But he kept quite quiet
About this diet.

Whenever William Cobbett
Saw a hen-roost, he would rob it.
He posed as a British Farmer,
But knew nothing about Karma.

[1] The line left blank has a series of secret symbols—quite
impossible to reproduce.

IRRESPONSIBLE OUTBREAK OF ONE WHO, HAVING COMPLETED A BOOK OF ENORMOUS LENGTH ON THE POET CHAUCER, FEELS HIMSELF FREED FROM ALL BONDS OF INTELLECTUAL SELF-RESPECT AND PROPOSES TO DO NO WORK FOR AN INDEFINITE PERIOD

"Wot ye not wher ther stout a litel toun,
Which that icleped is Bob-up-an-down."
—THE CANTERBURY TALES

They babble on of Babylon
They tire me out with Tyre
And Sidon putting side on
I do not much admire.
But the little town Bob-Up-and-Down
That lies beyond the Blee
Along the road our fathers rode,
O that's the town for me.

In dome and spire and cupola
It bubbles up and swells
For the company that canter
To the Canterbury Bells.
But when the Land Surveyors come
With maps and books to write,
The little town Bob-Up-and-Down
It bobs down out of sight.

I cannot live in Liverpool,
O lead me not to Leeds,
I'm not a Man in Manchester,
Though men be cheap as weeds:
But the little town Bob-Up-and-Down
That bobs towards the sea
And knew its name when Chaucer came,
O that's the town for me.

I'll go and eat my Christmas meat
In that resurgent town
And pledge to fame our Father's name

Till the sky bobs up and down;
And join in sport of every sort
That's played beside the Blee,
Bob-Apple in Bob-Up-and-Down,
O that's the game for me.

Now Huddersfield is Shuddersfield
And Hull is nearly Hell,
Where a Daisy would go crazy
Or a Canterbury Bell,
The little town Bob-Up-and-Down
Alone is fair and free;
For it can't be found above the ground,
O that's the place for me.

NURSERY RHYME

Little Jack Horner
Sat in a corner
Eating a Christmas pie;
He put in his thumb
And pulled out a plum,

And said: "My lords—ha! and ah—gentlemen—hum!
The conclusion to which the Committee has come
On the sociological residuum
Of the weak, the unfit, and the blind and the dumb—
The (in short) economic excrescence which some
In less technical terms have described as the Slum
Discovers a Nervous Prostration made numb
By the use of beer, brandy, gin, whisky, and rum,
Affecting the sensitive sensorium
With a blasting effect as of bullets (dum-dum);
And making our workers so gloomy and glum
That they can't take delight in the landscape of Brum,
And will seldom leap up like a chivalrous chum
To make somebody else's enterprise hum,
And receive in return, by a sound rule of thumb,
The more or less crumby proportion of crumb
Which falls from the table of Baron de Tum

Of Consolidate Glue and Incorporate Gum,
And the British Adventure in Bam-Buzalum.
The table all laden with Clicquot and Mumm
To which they might, too, have aspired, and become
Successful as we are: survived in the scrum
Of the fittest who fight for Honorarium,
And make in Imperio Imperium,
To the manifest gain of Lord Cockalorum;
And at last, to arrive at the Summum Bonum,
The evolving Eden and Elysium,
The Pattern of Fate with its thread and its thrum,
The End of Existence when—er—that is, um,
I appear; and the world has discarded its scum
Of ignorance, dirt, and of mere tedium,
And the beer and the bloodshed in which it has swum,
And the dissolute cask and the bellicose drum,
And the world that revolves like a mad teetotum
Round Me"—(or, to state his oration in sum)
He said: "What a good boy am I."

CLERIHEW

Savonarola
Did not wear a bowler.
He said man could not serve God and Mammon
But that was gammon.

ESKIMO SONG

"... So that the audience in Chicago will have the advantage
of hearing Eskimos singing." (or words to that effect)
—WIRELESS PROGRAMME.

Oh who would not want such a wonderful thing
As the pleasure of hearing the Eskimos sing?
I wish I had Eskimos out on the lawn,
Or perched on the window to wake me at dawn:
With Eskimos singing in every tree
Oh that would be glory, be glory for me!

Oh list to the song that the Eskimos sing,
When the penguin would be if he could on the wing,
Would soar to the sun if he could, like the lark,
But for most of the time it is totally dark.

Or hark to the bacchanal songs that resound
When they're making a night of it half the year round,
And carousing for months till the morning is pale,
Go home with the milk of the walrus and whale.

Oh list to the sweet serenades that are hers,
Who expensively gowned in most elegant furs,
Leans forth from the lattice delighted to know
That her heart is like ice and her hand is like snow.

*   *   *

God bless all the dear little people who roam
And hail in the icebergs the hills of their home;
For I might not object to be listening in
If I hadn't to hear the whole programme begin.
And the President preach international peace,
And Parricide show an alarming increase,
And a Justice at Bootle excuse the police,
And how to clean trousers when spotted with grease,
And a pianist biting his wife from caprice,
And an eminent Baptist's arrival at Nice,
And a banker's regrettably painless decease,
And the new quarantine for the plucking of geese,
And a mad millionaire's unobtrusive release,
And a marquis divorced by a usurer's niece—
If all of these items could suddenly cease
And leave me with one satisfactory thing
I really *should* like to hear Eskimos sing.

CLERIHEW

Thomas Carlyle
Has been forgotten all this while.
He wrote "Sartor Resartus,"
But that shan't part us.

FRIENDSHIP'S GARLAND

When I was a boy there was a friend of mine,
We thought ourselves warriors and grown folk swine,
Stupid old animals who never understood
And never had an impulse, and said "You must be good".

We stank like stoats and fled like foxes,
We put cigarettes in the pillar-boxes,
Lighted cigarettes and letters all aflame—
O the surprise when the postman came!

We stole eggs and apples and made fine hay
In people's houses when people were away,
We broke street lamps and away we ran;
Then I was a boy but now I am a man.

Now I am a man and don't have any fun,
I hardly ever shout and never never run,
And I don't care if he's dead, that friend of mine,
For then I was a boy and now I am a swine.

MIND AND MATTER

A gentleman, who lived at Ealing, taught—
"There is no limit to the power of thought."
'I still, however, can't help sometimes feeling
That thought alone does not account for Ealing.

AT EVENTIDE

Goo-goo goo-goo goo-goo goo
Goo-goo goo-goo goo-goo
Googly, googly, googly goo:
That's how we fill a column.

CLERIHEW

In reading Robert Burns
What a lot one learns.
He said a king could make a belted knight
And he was right.

PLAKKOPYTRIXOPHYLISPERAMBULANT-
IOBATRIX

A Twenty Minutes' Holiday from Writing Fiction.
12 p.m.

Fear not, fear not, my children,
The last weird embers fade,
Blue corpses through the windows peer,
But still you seem afraid,
Perhaps there's Something in the room,
Whatever would you do
If I were not among you now
To cheer and comfort you?

Heed not that pale thing in the door,
It smiles so like a skull,
You hear hoarse spectres scream and clank,
You find the evening dull?
Then let me tell a merry tale
Of dear old days of yore,
About a dragon of the wastes
That drank of human gore.

It dwelt among untrodden ways,
And ate the plaintive dove;
A dragon there were few to praise
And very few to love.
(I use this piece of Wordsworth
To show how much I know)
Uproariously popular
It was, as dragons go.

If I could only paint the Thing!
Just imitate its wink,
All you five infants, one by one,
Would rise and take to drink:
Or roll in death-pangs on the floor,
And lie there choked and blue,
O how I wish I could describe
This animal to you.

Some swore its fur was bushy brown,
Some swore that it was green,
With savage eyes of bluish grey:
Some swore that they had seen
In coils upon a sofa wreathed,
It, writhing as in pangs,
And tearing Bovril chocolate
With huge, abhorrent fangs.

Some said that far to eastward
They saw It, garbed in grey,
Standing upon a platform
And bellowing all day.
Some said that far to northward,
Through all the white snow-wreath,
They saw it, white and wolfish,
With half-a-million teeth.

When skies were blue with summer
It glittered, bright and blue,
And once, the stricken wanderer
In screaming terror flew,
For on the shining tableland
White gauze did round it glance,
And with one rose to crown it
He saw the dragon dance.

The Witless Youth in wonder
Sat lank upon a stone,
His Hat was monumental
Its secret—all his own.
The Sage was mild and hoary
And skilled in Wisdom's page,
The Youth sat meek (as always)
And to him spoke the Sage.

"Go not to smite the Dragon
That wasteth field and fen,
Around her reeking cavern
Are strewn the hearts of men;
But youth is foolish: You, Sir,
Are singularly so—
So learn her horrid habits
At least, before you go.

"If you would raise her bristles up
And set her eye in flames,
Then seek the Hankin-Pankin
And read the Jenry-James;

Go with a train of spiders huge
With all their threads and thrums
From ledgers all declaiming
Interminable sums . . .

"But would you see the awful smile,
And soften down the Eye,
Then fetch the Stompy-Steinthal
And bring the Rompy-Rye;
And choirs of ladies tall and proud
With all one kind of nose,
And bucketsful of flowers
And basketsful of clothes.'

(Unfinished, or if finished the last page has been lost.)

CLERIHEW

The novels of Jane Austen
Are the ones to get lost in.
I wonder if Labby
Has read "Northanger Abbey."

V

Chuck It, Smith!

Satirical verses

ON READING 'GOD'

(Mr. Middleton Murry explains that his
book with this title records his farewell
to god)

Murry, on finding *le Bon Dieu*
Chose difficile à croire
Illogically said "Adieu,"
But God said "Au Revoir."

ANTICHRIST, OR THE REUNION
OF CHRISTENDOM: AN ODE

"A Bill which has shocked the conscience of every
Christian community in Europe." —MR. F.E. SMITH,
on the Welsh Disestablishment Bill.

Are they clinging to their crosses,
      F.E. Smith,
Where the Breton boat-fleet tosses,
      Are they, Smith?
Do they, fasting, tramping, bleeding,
  Wait the news from this our city?
Groaning "That's the Second Reading!"
  Hissing "There is still Committee!"
If the voice of Cecil falters,
  If McKenna's point has pith,
Do they tremble for their altars?
      Do they, Smith?

Russian peasants round their pope
      Huddled, Smith,
Hear about it all, I hope,
      Don't they, Smith?
In the mountain hamlets clothing
  Peaks beyond Caucasian pales,
Where Establishment means nothing
  And they never heard of Wales,
Do they read it all in Hansard
  With a crib to read it with—
"Welsh Tithes: Dr. Clifford Answered."
      Really, Smith?

In the lands where Christians were,
                        F.E. Smith,
In the little lands laid bare,
                        Smith, O Smith,
Where the Turkish bands are busy,
        And the Tory name is blessed
Since they hailed the Cross of Dizzy
        On the banners from the West!
Men don't think it half so hard if
        Islam burns their kin and kith,
Since a curate lives in Cardiff
                        Saved by Smith.

It would greatly, I must own,
                        Soothe me, Smith!
If you left this theme alone,
                        Holy Smith!
For your legal cause or civil
        You fight well and get your fee;
For your God or dream or devil
        You will answer, not to me.
Talk about the pews and steeples
        And the Cash that goes therewith!
But the souls of Christian peoples . . .
                        —Chuck it, Smith!

COMFORT FOR COMMUNISTS

"In January of last year Bezboznik complained that anti-religious Soviets had
been disbanded in seventy districts, while it had been thought that in the
region of Kovrov there was a whole system of atheist cells, the President of
that region wrote . . . that neither in the town nor in the region were there any
cells left—in fact 'in the entire district there is now only one organised
atheist—myself.' "

                    —FROM AN ARTICLE BY FATHER C.C. MARTINDALE S.J.,
                        IN THE CATHOLIC HERALD, 11 MAY 1935.

"I'm all alone; I can't organise anyone,
There's nobody left to organise me,
And still I'm the only organised atheist
In all the province of Skuntz (E.C.).

Sometimes disgusting organised atheists
Orphan the stars without permit from me,
Unmake their Maker without their ticket
Or their copy of Form x.793.

The Blasphemy Drill's getting slacker and slacker,
Free Thought is becoming alarmingly free,
And I'll be the only organised atheist
Between the Bug and the big Black Sea."

*   *   *

Ours, ours is the key O desolate crier,
The golden key to what ills distress you
Left without ever a God to judge you,
Lost without even a Man to oppress you.

Look west, look west to the Land of Profits,
To the old gold marts, and confess it then
How greatly your great propaganda prospers
When left to the methods of Business Men.

Ah, Mammon is mightier than Marx in making
A goose-step order for godless geese,
And snobs know better than mobs to measure
Where Golf shall flourish and God shall cease.

Lift up your hearts in the wastes Slavonian,
Let no Red Sun on your wrath go down;
There are millions of very much organised atheists
In the Outer Circle of London town.

SONGS OF EDUCATION:

I. HISTORY
Form 991785, Sub-Section D

The Roman threw us a road, a road,
And sighed and strolled away:
The Saxon gave us a raid, a raid,
A raid that came to stay;
The Dane went west, but the Dane confessed
That he went a bit too far;
And we all became, by another name,
The Imperial race we are.

Chorus

The Imperial race, the inscrutable race,
The invincible race we are.

Though Sussex hills are bare, are bare,
And Sussex weald is wide,
From Chichester to Chester
Men saw the Norman ride;
He threw his sword in the air and sang
To a sort of a light guitar;
It was all the same, for we all became
The identical nobs we are.

Chorus

The identical nobs, individual nobs
Unmistakable nobs we are.

The people lived on the land, the land,
They pottered about and prayed;
They built a cathedral here and there
Or went on a small crusade:
Till the bones of Becket were bundled out
For the fun of a fat White Czar,
And we all became, in spoil and flame,
The intelligent lot we are.

Chorus

The intelligent lot, the intuitive lot,
The infallible lot we are.

O Warwick woods are green, are green,
But Warwick trees can fall:
And Birmingham grew so big, so big,
And Stratford stayed so small.
Till the hooter howled to the morning lark
That sang to the morning star;
And we all became, in freedom's name,
The fortunate chaps we are.

Chorus

The fortunate chaps, felicitous chaps,
The fairy-like chaps we are.

The people they left the land, the land,
But they went on working hard;
And the village green that had got mislaid
Turned up in the squire's backyard:
But twenty men of us all got work
On a bit of his motor car;
And we all became, with the world's acclaim,
The marvellous mugs we are:

Chorus

The marvellous mugs, miraculous mugs,
The mystical mugs we are.

II. Geography

Form 17955301, Sub-Section Z

The earth is a place on which England is found
And you find it however you twirl the globe round;
For the spots are all red and the rest is all grey,
And that is the meaning of Empire Day.

Gibraltar's a rock that you see very plain,
And attached to its base is the district of Spain.
And the island of Malta is marked further on,
Where some natives were known as the Knights of St. John.

Then Cyprus, and east to the Suez Canal,
That was conquered by Dizzy and Rothschild his pal
With the Sword of the Lord in the old English way;
And that is the meaning of Empire Day.

Our principal imports come far as Cape Horn;
For necessities, cocoa; for luxuries, corn;
Thus Brahmins are born for the rice-field, and thus,
The Gods made the Greeks to grow currants for us;
Of earth's other tributes are plenty to choose,
Tobacco and petrol and Jazzing and Jews:
The Jazzing will pass but the Jews they will stay;
And that is the meaning of Empire Day.

Our principal exports, all labelled and packed,
At the ends of the earth are delivered intact:
Our soap or our salmon can travel in tins
Between the two poles and as like as two pins;
So that Lancashire merchants whenever they like
Can water the beer of a man in Klondike
Or poison the meat of a man in Bombay;
And that is the meaning of Empire Day.

The day of St. George is a musty affair
Which Russians and Greeks are permitted to share;
The day of Trafalgar is Spanish in name
And the Spaniards refuse to pronounce it the same;
But the day of the Empire from Canada came
With Morden and Borden and Beaverbrook's fame

And saintly seraphical souls such as they.
And that is the meaning of Empire Day.

III. FOR THE CRÈCHE
Form 8277059, Sub-Section K

I remember my mother, the day that we met,
A thing I shall never entirely forget;
And I toy with the fancy that, young as I am,
I should know her again if we met in a tram.
   But mother is happy in turning a crank
   That increases the balance at somebody's bank;
   And I feel satisfaction that mother is free
   From the sinister task of attending to me.

They have brightened our room, that is spacious and cool,
With diagrams used in the Idiot School,
And Books for the Blind that will teach us to see;
But mother is happy, for mother is free.
   For mother is dancing up forty-eight floors,
   For love of the Leeds International Stores,
   And the flame of that faith might perhaps have grown cold,
   With the care of a baby of seven weeks old.

For mother is happy in greasing a wheel
For somebody else, who is cornering Steel;
And though our one meeting was not very long,
She took the occasion to sing me this song:

85

"O, hush thee, my baby, the time will soon come
When thy sleep will be broken with hooting and hum;
There are handles want turning and turning all day,
And knobs to be pressed in the usual way;

O, hush thee, my baby, take rest while I croon,
For Progress comes early, and Freedom too soon."

IV. CITIZENSHIP
Form 8889512, Sub-Section Q

How slowly learns the child at school
The names of all the nobs that rule
From Ponsonby to Pennant;
Ere his bewildered mind find rest,
Knowing his host can be a Guest,
His landlord is a Tennant.

He knew not, at the age of three,
What Lord St. Leger next will be
Or what he was before;
A Primrose in the social swim
A Mr. Primrose is to him,
And he is nothing more.

But soon, about the age of ten,
He finds he is a Citizen,
And knows hiw way about;
Can pause within, or just beyond,
The line 'twixt Mond and Demi-Mond,
'Twixt Getting On—or Out.

The Citizen will take his share
(In every sense) as bull and bear;
Nor need this oral ditty
Invoke the philologic pen
To show you that a Citizen
Means Something in the City.

Thus gains he, with the virile gown,
The fasces and the civic crown,

The forum of the free;
Not more to Rome's high law allied
Is Devonport in all his pride
Or Lipton's self than he.

For he will learn, if he will try,
The deep interior truths whereby
We rule the Commonwealth;
What is the Food-Controller's fee
And whether the Health Ministry
Are in it for their health.

V. THE HIGHER MATHEMATICS
Form 339125, Sub-Section M

Twice one is two,
　　Twice two is four,
But twice two is ninety-six if you know the way to score.
　　Half of two is one,
　　Half of four is two.
But half of four is forty per cent. if your name is Montagu:
For everything else is on the square
If done by the best quadratics;
And nothing is low in High Finance
Or the Higher Mathematics.

　　A straight line is straight
　　And a square mile is flat:
But you learn in trigonometrics a trick worth two of that.
　　Two straight lines
　　Can't enclose a Space,
But they can enclose a Corner to support the Chosen Race:
For you never know what Dynamics do
With the lower truths of Statics;
And half of two is a touring car
In the Higher Mathematics.

　　There is a place apart
　　Beyond the solar ray,
Where parallel straight lines can meet in an unofficial way.

There is a room that holds
The examiner or his clerks,
Where you can square the circle or the man that gives the marks.
Where you hide in the cellar and then look down
On the poets that live in the attics;
For the whole of the house is upside down
In the Higher Mathematics.

VI. HYGIENE
Form 394411102, Sub-Section X

"All practical eugenists are agreed on the importance of sleep."
—THE EUGENIC CONGRESS

When Science taught mankind to breathe
A little while ago,
Only a wise and thoughtful few
Were really in the know:
Nor could the Youth his features wreathe,
Puffing from all the lungs beneath:
When Duty whispered softly, "Breathe!"
The Youth would answer, "Blow!"

When Science proved with lucid care
The need of Exercise,
Our thoughtless Youth was climbing trees
Or lightly blacking eyes:
To reckless idlers breaking bounds
For football or for hare-and-hounds,
Or fighting hard for fourteen rounds,
It came as a surprise.

But when she boldly counsels sleep
To persons when in bed,
Then, then indeed men blush to see
The daybreak blushing red:
The early risers whom we term
Healthy, grow sickly and infirm;
The Early Bird who caught the Worm
Will catch the Germ instead.

For this at least be Science praised
If all the rest be rot,
That now she snubs the priggish child
That quits too soon his cot:
The pharisaic pachyderm
Of spiritual pride shall squirm:
The Early Bird catcheth the Worm,
The Worm that dieth not.

MEN LIKE GODS

Workers fly back and forth like piston-rods
And clerks like clocks strike eight or nine or ten:
Say, you who know when men will be like gods,
In what wild future men will be like men.

I THANK THE GOODNESS AND THE GRACE

Red guards for the Soviet, White guards for the Czar:
Thank God we live where only Blackguards are.

THE SONG OF THE SUPERIOR VERMIN

The little fleas have larger fleas upon their backs to bite,
Since Science found the latest type: the larger Parasite.

The little shops have bigger shops upon their backs to smash 'em,
Because they write the biggest cheques and banks will always cash 'em;
As Mr Wells he always tells, it will enlarge our Souls:
We used to call 'em Corners; now we call 'em World Controls.

The little states have bigger states upon their backs to break 'em,
And if the nations won't submit the Powers can always make 'em;
For three fat Empires sit on top to bully and intrigue;
It once was called a Concert, and now it's called a League.

The little banks have bigger banks upon their backs to boss 'em,
But anyhow the business man is treed like an opossum.
He cannot dig or pay or pray because he don't know how;
We used to call it Bankruptcy. What shall we call it now?

FUTURISTS' SONG

"We will sing the praises of man holding the flywheel of which the
ideal steering-post traverses the earth impelled itself around the
circuit of its own orbit."
                              —DECLARATION OF FUTURISM

A notion came into my head as new as it was bright
That poems might be written on the subject of a fight;
No praise was given to Lancelot, Achilles, Nap or Corbett,
But we will sing the praises of man holding the flywheel of
    which the ideal steering-post traverses the earth impelled
    itself around the circuit of its own orbit.

My fathers scaled the mountains in their pilgrimages far,
But I feel full of energy while sitting in a car;
And petrol is the perfect wine, I lick it and absorb it,
So we will sing the praises of man holding the flywheel of
    which the ideal steering-post traverses the earth impelled
    itself around the circuit of its own orbit.

TRUE SENSIBILITY

"A Russian woman would be quite offended if a man opened a door for her."

The Bolshevist lady is no less refined
    Than Victorian misses, but more.
They shrank if a man might be under the bed;
    She shrieks if he opens the door.

Though shirt-sleeves might shock them, the Bolshevist maid
    Is far more fastidious than that.
They frowned at a man if he took off his coat;
    She faints when he takes off his hat.

She blushes at anything all day long,
    Which is why it is commonly said
That while other young ladies are normally pink,
    She is now irretrievably Red.

THE HORRIBLE HISTORY OF JONES

Jones had a dog; it had a chain;
Not often worn, not causing pain;
But, as the I.K.L. had passed
Their "Unleashed Cousins Act" at last,
Inspectors took the chain away;
Whereat the canine barked "hurray!"
At which, of course, the S.P.U.
(Whose Nervous Motorists' Bill was through)
Were forced to give the dog in charge
For being Audibly at Large.

None, you will say, were now annoyed,
Save haply Jones—the yard was void.
But something being in the lease
About "alarms to aid police,"
The U.S.U. annexed the yard
For having no sufficient guard;
Now if there's one condition
The C.C.P. are strong upon
It is that every house one buys
Must have a yard for exercise;
So Jones, as tenant, was unfit,
His state of health was proof of it.
Two doctors of the T.T.U.'s
Told him his legs, from long disuse,
Were atrophied; and saying "So
From step to higher step we go
Till everything is New and True."
They cut his legs off and withdrew.
You know the E.T.S.T.'s views
Are stronger than the T.T.U.'s:
And soon (as one may say) took wing
The Arms, though not the Man, I sing.
To see him sitting limbless there
Was more than the K.K. could bear.
"In mercy silence with all speed
That mouth there are no hands to feed;
What cruel sentimentalist,
O Jones, would doom thee to exist—
Clinging to selfish Selfhood yet?
Weak one! Such reasoning might upset
The Pump Act, and the accumulation
Of all constructive legislation;
Let us construct you up a bit—"
The head fell off when it was hit:
Then words did rise and honest doubt,
And four Commissioners sat about
Whether the slash that left him dead
Cut off his body or his head.
An author in the Isle of Wight
Observed with unconcealed delight
A land of old and just renown
Where Freedom slowly broadened down

From Precedent to Precedent . . .
And this, I think, was what he meant.

A SONG OF MODERATION

They have said, the good and wise,
That it pays to advertise,
   And it's only right to speak with Moderation
Of a truth that stands so high,
Simply written on the sky,
   Though perhaps with just a touch of ostentation.

The beers that are best known
Are not arsenic alone,
   It is modified by salt and other things.
If you tell a waiter "And please
Will you bring some Gruyère cheese,"
   You can trifle with the substance that he brings.

There's a Port that you can drink,
And distinguish it from ink
   By a something that's not easy to define,
But not only from the poster
Of an after-dinner toaster
   Who has drunk enough to talk of it as wine.

The Yankee car is slick,
Put together very quick.
   When it comes apart with similar rapidity,
It will comfort you to know
It would take an hour or so
   To make it with Victorian solidity.

For it pays to advertise,
And when the engine lies
   On your stomach and the petrol's in a blaze,
And the car lies round you wrecked,
You'll have leisure to reflect
   Upon whom it is exactly that it pays.

THE LOGICAL VEGETARIAN

"Why shouldn't I have a purely vegetarian drink? Why shouldn't I take vegetables in their highest form, so to speak? The modest vegetarians ought obviously to stick to wine or beer, plain vegetarian drinks, instead of filling their goblets with the blood of bulls and elephants, as all conventional meat-eaters do, I suppose."

—DALROY

You will find me drinking rum,
　　Like a sailor in a slum,
You will find me drinking beer like a Bavarian
　　You will find me drinking gin
　　In the lowest kind of inn,
Because I am a rigid Vegetarian.

So I cleared the inn of wine,
　　And I tried to climb the sign,
And I tried to hail the constable as "Marion".
　　But he said I couldn't speak,
　　And he bowled me to the Beak
Because I was a Happy Vegetarian.

　　　*　　*　　*　　*　　*

I am silent in the Club,
　　I am silent in the pub.,
I am silent on a bally peak in Darien;
　　For I stuff away for life
　　Shoving peas in with a knife,
Because I am at heart a Vegetarian.

No more the milk of cows
Shall pollute my private house
Than the milk of the wild mares of the Barbarian;
I will stick to port and sherry,
For they are so very, very,
So very, very, very Vegetarian.

THE SIMPLE LIFE

The Chairman with a wig came in
(The one without a wig must go)
A metal club lay on the table
And not, as heretofore, below,

And when the Commons had reported,
And told themselves what they had done,
The Statesman of the simple faith
Came in to join the simple fun.

He sought the *left* side of the table,
Looking about him to make sure
His boots were not projecting over
A flat black mark upon the floor,

And then, replying to his nephew
(Whom he took care, of course, to call
The Honourable Member for
The Griles Division of Blackwall),

He promised measures to repress
Ritualistic Practices.

ON PROFESSOR FREUD

The ignorant pronounce it Frood,
To cavil or applaud.
The well-informed pronounce it Froyd,
But I pronounce it Fraud.

THE REVOLUTIONIST: OR, LINES TO A STATESMAN

"I was never standing by while a revolution was going on."

Speech by the RT. HON. WALTER LONG

When Death was on thy drums, Democracy,
And with one rush of slaves the world was free,
In that high dawn that Kings shall not forget,
A void there was and Walter was not yet.
Through sacked Versailles, at Valmy in the fray,
They did without him in some kind of way;
Red Christendom all Walterless they cross,
And in their fury hardly feel their loss . . .
Fades the Republic; faint as Roland's horn,
Her trumpets taunt us with a sacred scorn . . .
Then silence fell: and Mr. Long was born.

From his first hours in his expensive cot
He never saw the tiniest viscount shot.
In deference to his wealthy parents' whim
The mildest massacres were kept from him.
The wars that dyed Pall Mall and Brompton red
Passed harmless o'er that one unconscious head:
For all that little Long could understand
The rich might still be rulers of the land,
Vain are the pious arts of parenthood,
Foiled Revolution bubbled in his blood;
Until one day (the babe unborn shall rue it)
The Constitution bored him and he slew it.

If I were wise and good and rich and strong—
Fond, impious thought, if I were Walter Long—
If I could water sell like molten gold,
And make grown people do as they were told,
If over private fields and wastes as wide
As a Greek city for which heroes died,
I owned the houses and the men inside—
If all this hung on one thin thread of habit
I would not revolutionize a rabbit.

I would sit tight with all my gifts and glories,
And even preach to unconverted Tories,

That the fixed system that our land inherits,
Viewed from a certain standpoint, has its merits.
I'd guard the laws like any Radical,
And keep each precedent, however small,
However subtle, misty, dusty, dreamy,
Lest man by chance should look at me and see me;
Lest men should ask what madman made me lord
Of English ploughshares and the English sword;
Lest men should mark how sleepy is the nod
That drills the dreadful images of God!

Walter, be wise! avoid the wild and new!
The Constitution is the game for you.
Walter, beware! scorn not the gathering throng,
It suffers, yet it may not suffer wrong,
It suffers, yet it cannot suffer Long.
And if you goad it these grey rules to break,
For a few pence, see that you do not wake
Death and the splendour of the scarlet cap,
Boston and Valmy, Yorktown and Jemmappes,
Freedom in arms, the riding and the routing,
The thunder of the captains and the shouting,
All that lost riot that you did not share—
And when that riot comes—you *will* be there.

THE SHAKESPEARE MEMORIAL

Lord Lilac thought it rather rotten
That Shakespeare should be quite forgotten,
And therefore got on a Committee
With several chaps out of the City,
And Shorter and Sir Herbert Tree,
Lord Rothschild and Lord Rosebery,
And F.C.G. and Comyns Carr,
Two dukes and a dramatic star,
Also a clergyman now dead;
And while the vain world careless sped
Unheeding the heroic name—
The souls most fed with Shakespeare's flame
Still sat unconquered in a ring,
Remembering him like anything.

Lord Lilac did not long remain,
Lord Lilac did not come again.
He softly lit a cigarette
And sought some other social set
Where, in some other knots or rings,
People were doing cultured things,
—Miss Zwilt's Humane Vivarium
—The little men that paint on gum
—The exquisite Gorilla Girl. . . .
He sometimes, in this giddy whirl
(Not being really bad at heart),
Remembered Shakespeare with a start—
But not with that grand constancy
Of Clement Shorter, Herbert Tree,
Lord Rosebery and Comyns Carr
And all the other names there are;
Who stuck like limpets to the spot,
Lest they forgot, lest they forgot.

Lord Lilac was of slighter stuff;
Lord Lilac had had quite enough.

CLERIHEW

I deny that Mr. John Morley
Has, as so many suppose, a wall-eye.
I don't know that a rationalist
Is so very much worse than a nationalist.

THE JAZZ

A Study of Modern Dancing, in the manner of
Modern Poetry.

TLANNGERSHSHSH!
  Thrills of vibrant discord,
    Like the shivering of glass;
Some people dislike it; but I do not dislike it.
  I think it is fun,
Approximating to the fun
Of merely smashing a window;
But I am told that it proceeds
  From a musical instrument,
Or at any rate
  From an instrument.

  Black flashes . . .
. . . Flashes of intermittent darkness;
Somebody seems to be playing with the electric light;
  Some may possibly believe that modern dancing
  Looks best in the dark.

  I do not agree with them.
I have heard that modern dancing is barbaric,
  Pagan, shameless, shocking, abominable.
No such luck—I mean no such thing.
  The dancers are singularly respectable

  To the point of rigidity,
With something of the rotatory perseverance
  Of a monkey on a stick;

But there is more stick than monkey,
   And not, as slanderers assert,
More monkey than stick.

   Let us be moderate,
There are a lot of jolly people doing it,
   (Whatever it is),
Patches of joyful colour shift sharply,
   Like a kaleidoscope.
Green and gold and purple and splashes of splendid black,
   Familiar faces and unfamiliar clothes;
I see a nice-looking girl, a neighbour of mine, dancing.
   After all,
She is not very different;

She looks nearly as pretty as when she is not dancing . . .
. . . I see certain others, less known to me, also dancing.
They do not look very much uglier
   Than when they are sitting still.

(Bound, O Terpsichore, upon the mountains,
   With all your nymphs upon the mountains,
And Salome that held the heart of a king
   And the head of a prophet;
For to the height of this tribute
   Your Art has come.)

If I were writing an essay
—And you can put chunks of any number of essays
    Into this sort of poem—
I should say there was a slight disproportion
    Between the music and the dancing;
For only the musician dances
    With excitement,
While the dancers remain cold
    And relatively motionless
(Orpheus of the Lyre of Life
    Leading the forests in fantastic capers;
Here is your Art eclipsed and reversed,
    For I see men as trees walking).

If Mr. King stood on his head,
Or Mr. Simon butted Mr. Gray
    In the waistcoat,
Or the two Burnett-Browns
Strangled each other in their coat-tails,
    There would then be a serene harmony,
    A calm unity and oneness
    In the two arts.
    But Mr. King remains on his feet,
And the coat-tails of Mr. Burnett-Brown
    Continue in their customary position.

And something else was running in my head—
—Songs I had heard earlier in the evening;
    Songs of true lovers and tavern friends,
        Decent drunkenness with a chorus,
    And the laughter of men who could riot.
And something stirred in me;
    A tradition
Strayed from an older time,
    And from the freedom of my fathers:
That when there is banging, yelling and smashing to be done,
        I like to do it myself,
    And not delegate it to a slave,
        However accomplished.
And that I should sympathise,
        As with a revolt of human dignity,
If the musician had suddenly stopped playing,

And had merely quoted the last line
Of a song sung by Mrs. Harcourt Williams:
  "If you want any more, you must sing it yourselves."

THE WORLD STATE

OH, how I love Humanity,
  With love so pure and pringlish,
And how I hate the horrid French,
  Who never will be English!

The International Idea,
  The largest and the clearest,
Is welding all the nations now,
  Except the one that's nearest.

This compromise has long been known,
  This scheme of partial pardons,
In ethical societies
  And small suburban gardens—

The villas and the chapels where
  I learned with little labour
The way to love my fellow-man
  And hate my next-door neighbour.

REFUTATION OF THE ONLY TOO PREVALENT SLANDER THAT PARLIAMENTARY LEADERS ARE INDIFFERENT TO THE STRICT FULFIL-MENT OF THEIR PROMISES AND THE PRESERVATION OF THEIR REPUTATION FOR VERACITY

They said (when they had dined at Ciro's)
The land would soon be fit for heroes;
And now they've managed to ensure it,
For only heroes could endure it.

COMMERCIAL CANDOUR

(ON THE OUTSIDE OF A SENSATIONAL NOVEL IS PRINTED THE
STATEMENT: "THE BACK OF THE COVER WILL TELL YOU THE
PLOT")

Our fathers to creed and tradition were tied,
They opened a book to see what was inside,
And of various methods they deemed not the worst
Was to find the first chapter and look at it first.
And so from the first to the second they passed,
Till in servile routine they arrived at the last.
But a literate age, unbenighted by creed,
Can find on two boards all it wishes to read;
For the front of the cover shows somebody shot
And the back of the cover will tell you the plot.

Between, that the book may be handily padded,
Some pages of mere printed matter are added,
Expanding the theme, which in case of great need
The curious reader might very well read
With the zest that is lent to a game worth the winning,
By knowing the end when you start the beginning;
While our barbarous sires, who would read every word
With a morbid desire to find out what occurred
Went drearily drudging through Dickens and Scott.
But the back of the cover will tell you the plot.

The wild village folk in earth's earliest prime
Could often sit still for an hour at a time
And hear a blind beggar, nor did the tale pall
Because Hector must fight before Hector could fall:
Nor was Scheherazade required, at the worst,
To tell her tales backwards and finish them first;
And the minstrels who sang about battle and banners
Found the rude camp-fire crowd had some notion of manners.
Till Forster (who pelted the people like crooks,
The Irish with buckshot, the English with books),
Established the great educational scheme
Of compulsory schooling, that glorious theme.
Some learnt how to read, and the others forgot,
And the back of the cover will tell you the plot.

O Genius of Business! O marvellous brain,
Come in place of the priests and the warriors to reign!
O Will to Get On that makes everything go—
O Hustle! O Pep! O Publicity! O!
Shall I spend three-and-sixpence to purchase the book,
Which we all can pick up on the bookstall and look?
Well, it may appear strange, but I think I shall not,
For the back of the cover will tell you the plot.

SOME WISHES AT XMAS

Mince-pies grant Wishes: let each name his Prize,
But as for us, we wish for more Mince-Pies.

MR. EPSTEIN

What wish has Epstein's art portrayed?
    Toward what does Rima rise?
Those little hands were never made
    To tear out eagles' eyes:
She for Green Mansions yearns; but not
So green a mansion as she got.

DEAN INGE

What deep desires inspire the Gloomy Dean,
While Rima chants The Wearing of the Green?
Does he have childlike hopes at Christmas time
And sing a carol or a nursery rhyme?
Does he hang up a stocking—or a gaiter—
Or ask for gifts from any Alma Mater?
(Tell me, do Matthew, Mark, and Luke and John
Bless beds the Higher Critics lie upon?
Or if, while the Fourth Gospel is re-read,
"Synoptists" sleep on a three-cornered bed.)
Or, like the Deutero-Job, who far away
On his interpolated ash-heap lay,
Damns he the day whereon his body and soul
Escaped the vigilance of Birth-Control?
Or, softened while the herald angel sings,
Does he more mildly wish for lesser things
That warning cracks, marking the house that falls,
Should decorate St. Peter's, not St. Paul's;
Or wish in all good faith to friends held dear
A Gloomy Christmas and a Glum New Year?
A Merry Christmas to a Merrier Dean!
Whatever he may want, whatever mean,
He won't be happy till he gets it; when
He does, perhaps he won't be happy then.

She wants a new England, more bright and more clean,
Where foul tap-room revelries never are seen.
And after the quarter-staff flies the quart-pot,
For she wants a new England where these things are not,
And our love of old England is vain in her sight,
As the noise of blind drunkards that strive in the night,
As if our old England like fable could fade,
And a Puritan purge through the ages had made
A Shaker of Shakespeare, a grave man of Gay,
And a Pussyfoot Johnson with Boswell to play.
For she wants a new England, where censors and prigs
Can browbeat our jokes and can bridle our jigs.
The title is apt, and the tale is soon told,
She wants a New England, three hundred years old.

THE COMMUNISTS

There are two normal nuisances
    That stir us late or soon:
One is the man who wants the earth,
    The other wants the moon.
Choosing between these last and Jix,
    We much prefer the lunatics.

JIX

Since Christmas time brings charity
    For Jix and for the Kaiser,
We wish that they were wise enough
    To wish that they were wiser.

THE UTMOST FOR THE HIGHEST

"...Up, up, up; on, on, on." *—Remarkable summary*
of modern thought and evolutionary ethics by the RIGHT HON.
RAMSAY MACDONALD

Since we first were sold a pup,
Till these dead dogs' day is done,
Evolution up, up, up,
Evolutes us on, on, on.

Till we're sacked and left with tup-
-pence a week to live upon.
Mines will blow us up, up, up,
Coppers move us on, on, on.

Till we find the fatal cup
Full, and God's own patience gone,
Till it's plain that all is Up
They will always have us On.

CLERIHEWS

The Rev. Stopford Brooke
The Church forsook.
He preached about an apple
In Bedford Chapel.

When they christened Laurence Oliphant
He observed, "What a jolly font."
This irreverent remark
Was overheard by the Clerk.

It is a peculiarity of Ruskin
Never to wear a buskin.
I advise you to spend your pennies
On "The Stones of Venice."

THE NEW FREETHINKER

John Grubby, who was short and stout
And troubled with religious doubt,
Refused about the age of three
To sit upon the curate's knee;
(For so the eternal strife must rage
Between the spirit of the age
And Dogma, which, as is well known,
Does simply hate to be outgrown).
Grubby, the young idea that shoots,
Outgrew the ages like old boots;
While still, to all appearance, small,
Would have no Miracles at all;
And just before the age of ten
Firmly refused Free Will to men.
The altars reeled, the heavens shook,
Just as he read of in the book;
Flung from his house went forth the youth
Alone with tempests and the Truth,
Up to the distant city and dim
Where his papa had bought for him
A partnership in Chepe and Deer
Worth, say, twelve hundred pounds a year.
But he was resolute. Lord Brute
Had found him useful; and Lord Loot,
With whom few other men would act,
Valued his promptitude and tact;
Never did even philanthropy
Enrich a man more rapidly:
'Twas he that stopped the Strike in Coal,
For hungry children racked his soul;
To end their misery there and then
He filled the mines with Chinamen
Sat in that House that broke the Kings,
And voted for all sorts of things—
And rose from Under-Sec. to Sec.
With scarce a murmur or a check.
Some grumbled. Growlers who gave less
Than generous worship to success,
The little printers in Dundee,
Who got ten years for blasphemy,

(Although he let them off with seven)
Respect him rather less than heaven.
No matter. This can still be said:
Never to supernatural dread,
Never to unseen deity,
Did Sir John Grubby bend the knee;
Never did dream of hell or wrath
Turn Viscount Grubby from his path;
Nor was he bribed by fabled bliss
To kneel to any world but this.
The curate lives in Camden Town,
His lap still empty of renown,
And still across the waste of years
John Grubby, in the House of Peers,
Faces that curate, proud and free,
And never sits upon his knee.

THE JOYS OF SCIENCE

I took her and I flattened her
Respectfully, I hope——
I pasted her upon a slip
Under the microscope,
With six-power lens I spied her,
Ah, ne'er shall I forget,
While hearts can beat and flowers bloom,
That hour when first we met.

Oh with what prayers and fasting
Shall mortal man deserve
To see that glimpse of Heaven
Her motor vagus nerve.
Look not, ye too inflammable,
Beneath that harmless hair,
The convolutions of her brain
Are perilously fair.

I breathed into that microscope
A Vow of burning tone,
I swore by men and angels,

The thunder and the throne,
That ere one brave, brown hair were touched
On that triumphant head
My serum's red corpuscula
Should cheerfully be shed.

Spurn not the men of Science,
They sob beneath your sneers
As with their large thermometers
They test their burning tears,
Because they rend the rock and flower
To prove, is this their sin,
Nature, the good King's daughter,
All glorious within.

A CHRISTMAS CAROL

The Chief Constable has issued a statement de-
claring that carol singing in the streets by children
is illegal, and morally and physically injurious. He
appeals to the public to discourage the practice.
—DAILY PAPER

God rest you merry gentlemen,
Let nothing you dismay;
The Herald Angels cannot sing,
The cops arrest them on the wing,
And warn them of the docketing
Of anything they say.

God rest you merry gentlemen,
May nothing you dismay:
On your reposeful cities lie
Deep silence, broken only by
The motor horn's melodious cry,
The hooter's happy bray.

So, when the song of children ceased
And Herod was obeyed,
In his high hall Corinthian

With purple and with peacock fan,
Rested that merry gentleman;
And nothing him dismayed.

PERFECTION[1]

Of all the heroes whom the poets sing
The one I like is General Goering:
A man of iron, cold and stern, it seems,
Ask him the simplest question and he screams,
If any other witness moves or speaks
The Court-House rings with long protracted shrieks;
These sounds, mysterious to the racial stranger,
Impress an Aryan people with the danger
Of interrupting strong and silent men
Just at the psychological moment when
They are, for Reich, Race, Goering and Gore,
Having hysterics on the Court-House floor:
Howl at us, black and purple in the face,
To note the calm of the Germanic race.

Not oft to any council, crowd or king,
Comes the high windfall of the Perfect Thing.
Those that dwell nearest Music's mightiest chords
Think the best German Songs are Without Words
Or, studying Heine's soul, may ponder long
How such a sneer became a Perfect Song:
Hitlerites may explain how Race can teach
Imperfect wits to make a Perfect Speech,
But all who know what crowns our mortal dream
Will own that Goering is a Perfect Scream.

[1] The world will not forget the weird psychological effect of the Prime Minister of Prussia shouting at a prisoner supposed to be receiving a fair trial, "You wait till I get you outside" like a very low-class schoolboy threatening what he would do out of school. That sort of thing simply does not happen among civilised people: not even when they are very wicked people. How anybody can see such lunacy dancing in high places, in the broad daylight of political responsibility, and have any further doubt about the sort of danger that threatens the world, is more than I can understand.
—G.K.C. (1933)

THE NEW FICTION

"Leave them alone," we seem to hear Mr. Galsworthy
say of his young people.

—FROM A REVIEW BY MR. BETTANY

Little Blue-Fits has lost his wits,
    And doesn't know where to find them;
Leave them alone and they'll come home,
    And leave their tales behind them.

The remarkable tales, with remarkable sales,
    And Bonnets and Bees in disorder;
For the Bonnets we view are exceedingly Blue,
    And decidedly over the Border.

AN ALPHABET

A   is an Agnostic dissecting a frog,
B   was a Buddhist who had been a dog,
C   was a Christian, a Christist I mean,
D   was the Dog which the Buddhist had been,
E   is for Ethics that grow upon trees,
F   for St. Francis who preached to the fleas,
G   is for God which is easy to spell,
H   is for Haeckel and also for Hell,
I   is for Incas now commonly dead,
J   is a Jesuit under the bed,
K   is the letter for Benjamin Kidd,
    The Angels and Devils said don't, but he did
L   Louis the Ninth who unlike the Eleventh,
    Was a much better man than King Edward the Seventh.
M is for Man, by the way, what is Man?
N   is for Nunquam who'll tell if he can,
O   is the Om about which I won't trouble you,
P   for the Pope and P.W.W.[1]
Q   is the Quaker quiescent in quod,

---

[1] P.W.W. was P.W. Wilson, a colleague of Chesterton's on *The Daily News*.

R   is for Reason, a primitive God,
S   is the Superman, harmless but fat,
T   a Theosophist losing his hat,
U   the Upanishads, clever but slight,
V   is a Virtuous Man killing Beit,[2]
W   is for Wesley who banged with his fist,
X   for King Xerxes, a monotheist,
Y   is for You who depraved as you are,
    Are Lord of Creation and Son of a Star.
Z   Zarathustra who couldn't take stout,
    He made war on the weak and they banged him about.

CLERIHEWS

Lord Rosebery
In the Foreign Office papers would his nose
    bury;
But you are not to suppose
That he was ashamed of his nose.

Doctor Parker
Was no relation to T'Chaka.
He wrote to the "Times";
But that was the least his crimes.

[2] Alfred Beit was a Hamburg-born financier (reputedly the world's richest man) whose wealth came from South Africa and whom Chesterton loathed. He is the subject of this clerihew by Bentley: Mr Alfred Beit/Screamed suddenly in the night./When they asked him why/He made no reply.

A BROAD-MINDED BISHOP REBUKES
THE VERMINOUS ST. FRANCIS

If Brother Francis pardoned Brother Flea,
There still seems need of such strange charity,
Seeing he is, for all his gay goodwill,
Bitten by funny little creatures still.

TO A HOLY ROLLER
(The Sect of the Holy Rollers demonstrated against
Evolution at Dayton)

"Roll on," said Gilbert to the earth:
   "Roll on," said Byron to the sea:
Accepting natural features thus,
   Freely I say "Roll on" to thee.

Time like an ever rolling stream
   Bears his most rolling sons away
Bryanite saint, Darwinian sage,
   And even Dayton has its day.

Earth changes; sings another bard,
   "There rolls the deep where grew the tree";
Convulsions viewed with equal calm
   By Tennyson and Tennessee.

But ere you roll down history's slope,
    A moment you may set us thinking
How Prohibition suits their mood,
    Who get so drunk by never drinking.

What rows of bottles, blends of liquor,
    We need to reach in one wild leap
Those reels and rolls you get for nothing,
    Great Bacchic Maenads on the cheap!

I blame you not that, writhing prone,
    You flout the grave Darwinian's view,
Of his extremely Missing Link,
    For he is quite amusing too.

Marking the human ape evolve
    (He puts his rolling into Latin),
Through epochs barely large enough
    To swing an old Egyptian cat in.

Since you believe Man truly tilled
    The Garden for the great Controller,
You back your Garden party up,
    Like a consistent Garden Roller.

We, too, may deem on Adam's birth
    Some more mysterious splendour shone,
Than prigs can pick off monkey's bones,
    Never you mind! Roll on! Roll on!

Grovel and gambol on all fours
    Till you have proved beyond dispute
That human dignity is freed
    From all connection with the brute.

CLERIHEW

Mr Henry Irving
Was most unnerving.
He uttered strange yells
In "The Bells."

RACE-MEMORY

(By a dazed Darwinian)

I remember, I remember
  Long before I was born,
The tree-tops where my racial self
  Went dancing round at morn.

Green wavering archipelagos,
  Great gusty bursts of blue,
In my race-memory I recall
  (Or I am told I do).

In that green-turreted Monkeyville
  (So I have often heard)
It seemed as if a Blue Baboon
  Might soar like a Blue Bird.

Low crawling Fundamentalists
  Glared up through the green mist,
I hung upon my tail in heaven
  A Firmamentalist.

        *   *   *

I am too fat to climb a tree,
  There are no trees to climb;
Instead, the factory chimneys rise,
  Unscaleable, sublime.

The past was bestial ignorance:
  But I feel a little funky,
To think I'm further off from heaven
  Than when I was a monkey.

CLERIHEW

James Hogg
Kept a dog,
But, being a shepherd
He did not keep a leopard.

THE HIGHER UNITY

"The Rev. Isaiah Bunter has disappeared into the interior of the Solomon Islands, and it is feared that he may have been devoured by the natives, as there has been a considerable revival of religious customs among the Polynesians."

—A REAL PARAGRAPH FROM A REAL PAPER; ONLY THE NAMES ALTERED

It was Isaiah Bunter
　Who sailed to the world's end,
And spread religion in a way
　That he did not intend.

He gave, if not the gospel-feast,
　At least a ritual meal;
And in a highly painful sense
　He was devoured with zeal.

And who are we (as Henson says)
　That we should close the door?
And should not Evangelicals
　All jump at shedding Gore?

And many a man will melt in man,
　Becoming one, not two,
When smacks across the startled earth
　The Kiss of Kikuyu.

When Man is the Turk, and the Atheist,
　Essene, Erastian Whig,
And the Thug and the Druse and the Catholic
　And the crew of the Captain's gig.

THE ARISTOCRAT

The Devil is a gentleman, and asks you down to stay
At his little place at What'sitsname (it isn't far away).
They say the sport is splendid; there is always something new,
And fairy scenes, and fearful feats that none but he can do;
He can shoot the feathered cherubs if they fly on the estate,
Or fish for Father Neptune with the mermaids for a bait;
He scaled amid the staggering stars that precipice, the sky,
And blew his trumpet above heaven, and got by mastery
The starry crown of God Himself, and shoved it on the shelf;
But the Devil is a gentleman, and doesn't brag himself.

O blind your eyes and break your heart and hack your hand away,
And lose your love and shave your head; but do not go to stay
At the little place in What'sitsname where folks are rich and clever;
The golden and the goodly house, where things grow worse for ever;
There are things you need not know of, though you live and die in
    vain,
There are souls more sick of pleasure than you are sick of pain;
There is a game of April Fool that's played behind its door,
Where the fool remains for ever and the April comes no more,
Where the splendour of the daylight grows drearier than the dark,
And life droops like a vulture that once was such a lark:
And that is the Blue Devil that once was the Blue Bird;
For the Devil is a gentleman, and doesn't keep his word.

WHEN I CAME BACK TO FLEET STREET

When I came back to Fleet Street,
  Through a sunset nook at night,
And saw the old Green Dragon
  With the windows all alight,
And hailed the old Green Dragon
  And the Cock I used to know,
Where all good fellows were my friends
  A little while ago;

I had been long in meadows,
  And the trees took hold of me,
And the still towns in the beech-woods,
  Where men were meant to be.
But old things held; the laughter,
  The long unnatural night,
And all the truth they talk in hell,
  And all the lies they write.

For I came back to Fleet Street,
  And not in peace I came;
A cloven pride was in my heart,
  And half my love was shame.
I came to fight in fairy tale,
  Whose end shall no man know—
To fight the old Green Dragon
  Until the Cock shall crow!

Under the broad bright windows
  Of men I serve no more,
The groaning of the old great wheels
  Thickened to a throttled roar:
All buried things broke upward;
  And peered from its retreat,
Ugly and silent, like an elf,
  The secret of the street.

They did not break the padlocks,
  Or clear the wall away.
The men in debt that drank of old

Still drink in debt to-day;
Chained to the rich by ruin,
  Cheerful in chains, as then
When old unbroken Pickwick walked
  Among the broken men.

Still he that dreams and rambles
  Through his own elfin air,
Knows that the street's a prison,
  Knows that the gates are there:
Still he that scorns or struggles
  Sees, frightful and afar,
All that they leave of rebels
  Rot high on Temple Bar.

All that I loved and hated,
  All that I shunned and knew,
Clears in broad battle lightning,
  Where they, and I, and you,
Run high the barricade that breaks
  The barriers of the street,
And shout to them that shrink within,
  The Prisoners of the Fleet.

CLERIHEW

Mr. William Whitely
Was most unsightly.
He sold nothing but cyder
And called that being a Universal Provider.

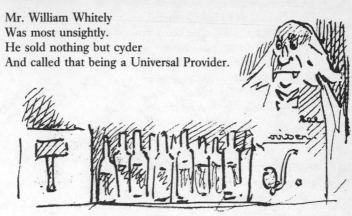

BIRTH CONTROL

The middle class their numbers find,
Compared with others, much declined:
And so the lower order ought
Compulsorily to be taught
The ingenious filth which brings to pass
The rotting of the middle class.

EDUCATION

Tom, Tom, the piper's son,
Learned that pipers' days are done
Since oaten pipe and pastoral song
To rude and rural scenes belong;
And all the tune that he could play
Was *Over the hills and far away.*

The Schools receive him; and he reads
The round of all our real needs;
The daylight hope of liberal days,
One life to live, one world to praise,
The life that ends where it began—
Here in the market-place of man:

They bid him trace in wheel and star
The God of all things as they are:
They called the laurelled lords of fame
To put his petty pipe to shame:
And rock-hewn Homer's hornèd lyre
And Maro's harp of heart's desire
Moaned with the tears of mortal things,
And Shakespeare clashed his thousand strings,
Crying and replying like a crowd;
And Dante's iron lute was loud
With high unhuman love and hate—
—At the calm signal of the State
And just enactment of the School
They drowned the piping of the fool.

But all the tune that they could play
Was *Over the hills and far away.*

VI

I Think I Will Not Hang Myself Today

The collected ballades

A BALLADE OF SUICIDE

The gallows in my garden, people say,
  Is new and neat and adequately tall;
I tie the noose on in a knowing way
  As one that knots his necktie for a ball;
  But just as all the neighbours—on the wall—
Are drawing a long breath to shout "Hurray!"
  The strangest whim has seized me.... After all
I think I will not hang myself to-day.

To-morrow is the time I get my pay—
  My uncle's sword is hanging in the hall—
I see a little cloud all pink and grey—
  Perhaps the rector's mother will not call—
  I fancy that I heard from Mr. Gall
That mushrooms could be cooked another way—
  I never read the works of Juvenal—
I think I will not hang myself to-day.

The world will have another washing-day;
  The decadents decay; the pedants pall;
And H.G. Wells has found that children play,
  And Bernard Shaw discovered that they squall,
  Rationalists are growing rational—
And through thick woods one finds a stream astray
  So secret that the very sky seems small—
I think I will not hang myself to-day.

ENVOI

Prince, I can hear the trumpet of Germinal,
The tumbrils toiling up the terrible way;
  Even to-day your royal head may fall,
I think I will not hang myself to-day.

BALLADE TO AN IRISHMAN

(With acknowledgments to L.J.M.)

For verse, and for the long ago,
   The game we played at (pretty dears)
When some of us were clever (oh!)
   And all of us were modern (cheers),
   When Pioneers, O Pioneers,
Stuck in the mud in various ways—
   I drink to Ireland down the years
To thine and mine and better days.

Even then, at least, we did not go
   With them that lent their lengthy ears
To Pigott, Carson, Nark and Co.;
   Not then preferred the snivelling sneers
   Of damned and putrid profiteers
(If I may be allowed the phrase)
   To justice and the great arrears,
To thine and mine and better days.

And now St. George's shield can show
   Not shamed with them that were his peers,
And on us too such daybreak glow
   As shows your dying Fusiliers,
   Borne high above the breaking spears
The Breastplate of St. Patrick blaze;
   Cry, for a cleaner England hears,
To thine and mine and better days.

ENVOI

Prince, trust me, even Mr. Squeers
Will only pummel while it pays:
   And Carsons look for no careers
To thine and mine and better days.

A BALLADE OF AN IMPARTIAL PERSON

'Mr Justice — concurred.' —LAW REPORT

They brought in Bills to boil the sea,
   They brought in Bills to burn the town,
To train a cow to climb a tree,
   To teach the fishes how to drown,
   They hanged the Harlequin and Clown
For being knowingly absurd;
   They fined assassins half a crown;
And Mr. Justice Brown concurred.

They mixed the views of Locke, Legree,
   Burke, Shylock, Cobden and Calhoun,
They choked the labour of the free
   In yellow mud from Chinatown;
   We broke our blade of clear renown,
We broke our bank, we broke our word,
   But Britain's statesmen did not frown
And Mr. Justice Brown concurred.

Sweet is such antique loyalty.
  Quaint as the rhymes of Ercildoune—
It was decided formally
  By the advisers of the Crown,
  To give to Mr. Justice Brown
(Unless a peerage was preferred)
  Say fifteen hundred thousand down—
And Mr. Justice Brown concurred.

ENVOI

  Prince, when you spoke in cap and gown,
You let it plainly be inferred
  You thought that "possum" was a noun—
—And Mr. Justice Brown concurred.

BALLADE OF A MORBID MODERN
(after reading many reminiscences)

I shun my kind. In shame I hang my head
  When Giggles takes me to the Plotless Play;
I dread my dreadful secret may be read
  At the *Green Toad*, the *Gripes*, the old *Death-Ray*,
  The *Nightmare Night-Club;* blind I stare and say
As old Rankeillor to his servant Torrance
  (What, you read *Stevenson* . . . hush! Whispers pray)
I'm getting rather tired of D.H. Lawrence.

Oh what he said she said they said he said!
  Oh what she says he said she said they say!
. . . We are grown men; and born and bred and wed
  Not quite in sunder from the common clay;
  We read plain words with which the street-boys play
Without much admiration or abhorrence
  But what the devil does it *matter* . . . eh?
I'm getting rather tired of D.H. Lawrence.

Not mightier are the minds in being misled
  Who miss the front-door or mistake the day

And break through gutters and back-drains instead;
   Perhaps the only way—but not the way.
   Nor mock I dirt or doubt or disarray,
But when their gutters flood the house in torrents
   (a modern rhyme) I mention, if I may,
I'm getting rather tired of D.H. Lawrence.

ENVOI

   Prince, *fortes ante Agamemnona*,
A man named Alighieri lived in Florence
   And William Shakspur lived down Warwick way—
I'm getting rather tired of D.H. Lawrence.

A BALLADE OF THE FIRST RAIN

The sky is blue with summer and the sun,
   The woods are brown as autumn with the tan,
It might as well be Tropics and be done,
   I might as well be born a copper Khan;
   I fashion me an oriental fan
Made of the wholly unreceipted bills
   Brought by the ice-man, sleeping in his van
(A storm is coming on the Chiltern Hills).

I read the Young Philosophers for fun
   —Fresh as our sorrow for the late Queen Anne—
The Dionysians whom a pint would stun,
   The Pantheists who never heard of Pan:
   —But through my hair electric needles ran,
And on my book a gout of water spills
   And on the skirts of heaven the guns began,
A storm is coming on the Chiltern Hills.

O fields of England, cracked and dry and dun,
   O soul of England, sick of words and wan,
The clouds grow dark; the down-rush has begun;
   —It comes, it comes, as holy darkness can,
   Black as with banners, ban and arrière-ban;
A falling laughter all the valley fills,

Deep as God's thunder and the thirst of man,
A storm is coming on the Chiltern Hills.

Prince, Prince-Elective on the modern plan,
Fulfilling such a lot of People's Wills,
    You take the Chiltern Hundreds while you can,
A storm is coming on the Chiltern Hills.

A BALLADE OF THE GROTESQUE

I was always the Elephant's Friend,
    I never have caused him to grieve;
Though monstrous and mighty to rend
    He was fed from the fingers of Eve,
    He is wise, but he will not deceive,
He is kind in his wildest career;
    But still I will say, with his leave,
The shape is decidedly queer.

I was light as a penny to spend,
   I was thin as an arrow to cleave,
I could stand on a fishing-rod's end,
   With composure, though on the *qui vive*,
   But from Time, all a-flying to thieve
The suns and the moons of the year,
   A different shape I receive;
The shape is decidedly queer.

I am proud of the world as I wend,
   What hills could Omnipotence heave,
I consider the heaven's blue bend
   A remarkable feat to achieve;
   —But think of the Cosmos—conceive
The universe—system and sphere,
   I must say with my heart on my sleeve,
The shape is decidedly queer.

ENVOI

   Prince, Prince, what is this I perceive
On the top of your collar appear?
   You say it's your face, you believe,
. . . The shape is decidedly queer.

A BALLADE OF EPHEMERAL CONTROVERSY

I am not as that Poet that arrives,
   Nor shall I pluck the laurel that persists
Through all perverted ages and revives:
   Enough for me, that if with feet and fists
   I fought these pharisaic atheists,
I need not crawl and seek when all is done
   My motley pennon trampled in the lists
It will not matter when the fight is won.

If scratch of mine amid a war of knives
   Has caused one moment's pain to pessimists,
Poisoned one hour in Social Workers' lives,
   I count such comfort more than amethysts

But less than claret, and at after trysts
We'll meet and drink such claret by the tun
    Till you and I and all of us (What? Hists!).
It will not matter when the fight is won.

When men again want women for their wives,
    And even woman owns that she exists,
When people ask for houses and not hives
    When we have climbed the tortured ivy's twists
    To where like statues stand above the mists
The strong incredible sanities in the sun,
    This dazed and overdriven bard desists.
It will not matter when the fight is won.

ENVOI

Prince, let me place these handcuffs on your wrists
While common Christian people get some fun,
    Then go and join your damned Theosophists.
It will not matter when the fight is won.

BALLADE D'UNE GRANDE DAME

Heaven shall forgive you Bridge at dawn,
    The clothes you wear—or do not wear—
And Ladies' Leap-frog on the lawn
    And dyes and drugs and *petits verres*.
    Your vicious things shall melt in air . . .
. . . But for the Virtuous Things you do,
    The Righteous Work, the Public Care,
It shall not be forgiven you.

Because you could not even yawn
    When your Committees would prepare
To have the teeth of paupers drawn,
    Or strip the slums of Human Hair;
    Because a Doctor Otto Maehr
Spoke of "a segregated few"—
    And you sat smiling in your chair—
It shall not be forgiven you.

Though your sins cried to—Father Vaughan,
  These desperate you could not spare
Who steal, with nothing left to pawn;
  You caged a man up like a bear
  For ever in a jailer's care
Because his sins were more than *two* . . .
  . . . I know a house in Hoxton where
It shall not be forgiven you.

ENVOI

  Princess, you trapped a guileless Mayor
To meet some people that you knew . . .
  When the last trumpet rends the air
It shall not be forgiven you.

BALLADE OF A PERIODICAL

In icy circles by the Behring Strait,
    In moony jungles where the tigers roar,
In tropic isles where civil servants wait,
    And wonder what the deuce they're waiting for,
    In lonely lighthouses beyond the Nore,
In English country houses crammed with Jews,
    Men still will study, spell, perpend and pore
And read the *Illustrated London News*.

Our fathers read it at the earlier date
    And twirled the funny whiskers that they wore
Ere little Levy got his first estate
    Or Madame Patti got her first encore.
    While yet the cannon of the Christian tore
The lords of Delhi in their golden shoes
    Men asked for all the news from Singapore
And read the *Illustrated London News*.

But I, whose copy is extremely late
    And ought to have been sent an hour before,
I still sit here and trifle with my fate
    And idly write another ballade more.
    I know it is too late; and all is o'er,
And all my writings they will now refuse,
    I shall be sacked next Monday. So be sure
And read the *Illustrated London News*.

ENVOI

Prince, if in church the sermon seems a bore
Put up your feet upon the other pews,
    Light a Fabrica de Tabagos Flor
And read the *Illustrated London News*.

BALLADE OF KINDNESS TO MOTORISTS

O Motorists, Motorists, run away and play,
　　I pardon you. Such exercise resigned, .
When would a statesman see the woods in May?
　　How could a banker woo the western wind?
　　When you have knocked a dog down I have pined,
When you have kicked the dust up I have sneezed,
　　These things come from your absence—well, of Mind—
But when you get a puncture I am pleased.

I love to see you sweating there all day
　　About some beastly hole you cannot find;
While your poor tenants pass you in a dray,
　　Or your sad clerks bike by you at a grind,
　　I am not really cruel or unkind;
I would not wish you mortally diseased,
　　Or deaf or dumb or dead or mad or blind,
But when you get a puncture I am pleased.

What slave that dare not smile when chairs give way?
　　When smart boots slip, having been lately shined?
When curates cannon with the coffee tray?
　　When trolleys take policemen from behind?
　　When kings come forth in public, having dined,
And palace steps are just a trifle greased?—
　　The joke may not be morbidly refined,
But when you get a puncture I am pleased.

ENVOI

　　Prince of the Car of Progress Undefined,
On to your far Perfections unappeased!
　　Leave your dead past with its dead children lined;
But when you get a puncture I am pleased.

VISION IN BEDFORD PARK

Bedford Parkers see a Dreadful Vision of the Future: an old acquaintance going to Church.

BALLADE OF BEDFORD PARK

Dear Olga, it was Long Ago,
  If life may be accounted long,
When by the windows (often bow)
  Or on the stairways (seldom strong)
  Summoned (perhaps) by copper gong
Fixed up by Craftsmen pure and stark,
  We met in that amazing throng
People we met in Bedford Park.

There was a velvet black-haired beau
  I could have murdered (which is wrong),
There was a lady trailing slow
  Enormous draperies along.
  And there was Yeats: not here belong
Sneers at the stir that made us mark
  That heathen but heroic song—
—People we met in Bedford Park.

But some friends stay and some friends go
  And we at least remain too long:
God knows if Boston or Hong-Kong
  Holds Doctor Jack or Mr Coe
  And there were others . . . stop . . . What ho!
Now I remember to remark—
  Why, there was Frances, too, among
People we met in Bedford Park.

ENVOI

  Princess, we both have come to know
What might have proved a happier Ark
  For Hankin and for Yeats and Co.,
People we knew in Bedford Park.

BALLADE OF DEVASTATION[1]

They're breaking down the bridge at Waterloo;
    They've daubed the house of Henry James at Rye;
They've caught a man and put him in the zoo;
    They've let the Japanese into Shanghai;
    They may destroy St. Peter's (on the sly);
They all agree that dogma has to go;
    From pole to pole the shattered temples lie;
They're cutting down the trees in Cheyne Row.

Who are these Vandals, these accursed Hoo?
    Powers that destroy and spirits that deny?
(You'll find their recreations in Who's Who)
    Those who would splash their liquors in the sky,
    And drench the stars in artificial dye;
They wallow in the wide world's overthrow;
    They would uplift the ultimate blasphemy;
They're cutting down the trees in Cheyne Row.

Carlyle complained of Chelsea cows that moo,
    Where old world lavender is still the cry,
Where Whistler's wizard dreams in green and blue
    Rest on the unresting river drifting by;
    "The King and Bells" is closing early . . . why?
Where you and I . . . but that was long ago . . .
    They say that the whole world is going dry . . .
They're cutting down the trees in Cheyne Row.

ENVOI

    Prince, they've abolished God in Muscovy;
You think that you are safe. That is not so.
    Much greater things than you are doomed to die:
They're cutting down the trees in Cheyne Row.

[1] By G.K.C. and Maurice Baring.

A BALLADE OF A BOOK-REVIEWER

I have not read a rotten page
  Of "Sex-Hate" or "The Social Test",
And here comes "Husks" and "Heritage";
  O Moses, give us all a rest!
  "Ethics of Empire"! . . . I protest
I will not even cut the strings,
  I'll read "Jack Redskin on the Quest"
And feed my brain with better things.

Somebody wants a Wiser Age
  (He also wants me to invest),
Somebody likes the Finnish stage
  Because the jesters do not jest;
  And grey with dust is Dante's crest,
The bell of Rabelais soundless swings:
  And the winds come out of the west
And feed my brain with better things.

Lord of our laughter and our rage,
  Look on us with our sins oppressed!
I too have trodden mine heritage
  Wickedly wearying of the best.
  Burn from my brain and from my breast
Sloth, and the cowardice that clings
  And stiffness and the soul's arrest;
And feed my brain with better things.

ENVOI

Prince, you are host and I am guest,
Therefore I shrink from cavillings,
  But I should have that fizz suppressed
And feed my brain with better things.

A BALLADE OF THEATRICALS

Though all the critics' canons grow—
  Far seedier than the actors' own—
Although the cottage-door's too low—
  Although the fairy's twenty stone—
  Although, just like the telephone,
She comes by wire and not by wings,
  Though all the mechanism's known—
Believe me, there are real things.

Yes, real people—even so—
  Even in a theatre, truth is known,
Though the agnostic will not know,
  And though the gnostic will not own,
  There is a thing called skin and bone,
And many a man that struts and sings
  Has been as stony-broke as stone . . .
Believe me, there are real things.

There is an hour when all men go;
  An hour when Man is quite alone.
When idle minstrels in a row
  Went down with all the bugles blown—

When brass and hymn and drum went down,
Down in death's throat with thunderings—
  Ah, though the unreal things have grown,
Believe me, there are real things.

  Prince, though your hair is not your own
And half your face held on by strings,
  And if you sat, you'd smash your throne—
—Believe me, there are real things.

A BALLADE OF REASONABLE INQUIRY

I—NATURAL RELIGION

Why is my head covered with curious hairs?
  Why does bread come out of a lot of yeast?
Why do male horses always mate with mares?
  Why have the baby's measurements increased?
  My own extension has abruptly ceased.
Why Huxley charms, but Hæckel makes me tired?
  Why is the sun still rising in the East?
I think an explanation is required.

II—SUPERNATURAL RELIGION

Whence all the tales of dreams and answered prayers?
  Whence flowed the wine at Cana's wineless feast?
How do they make a table walk upstairs?
  Why do I meet my uncle, now deceased?
  ... Yes ... doubtless ... as you truly say, the priest
Forced on a darkened world by fear inspired
  Warped explanations ... but to say the least,
I think an explanation is required.

III—POLITICS AND SOCIOLOGY

How long will empires swarm with bulls and bears?
  And men feel rather proud of being fleeced?
When Sergeant Sheridan sought balmier airs,

How were the wheels of his wild chariot greased?
When those Raid wires were pawed about and pieced,
What was that wire whose text has not transpired?
Now Chartereds have so painfully decreased,
I think an explanation is required.

Prince, now about this hare on which we feast,
Fitzsimmons swears you never even fired,
And Dick declares you never saw the beast,
I think an explanation is required.

BALLADE OF AN OLD MAN[1]

O you that measure all things long—
    Long views, long credit and long sight,
Cyrano's nose, Corelli's tongue,
    The pedigree of Otto Beit,[2]
    Who tell us how a star's far light
Crawls to us through eternity;
    Measure the time and mark the night
When first this book was lent to me.

---

[1] Inscribed in a book borrowed from Miss D. Childs, at whose home
Chesterton was a frequent visitor. [2] See 'An Alphabet'.

O long ago and lost among
  The rushing years in rout and flight,
When I was graceful, slim and strong
  And very like a Norman knight;
  My collar did not feel so tight,
My trousers bagged not at the knee:
  I was a lovely, lovely sight,
When first this book was lent to me.

Then wine was going for a song—
  And songs were easier to write;
And every nasty guess was wrong
  And every pleasant view was right:
  And all men spoke as well as Bright
And acted twice as well as Tree,
  And sour was sweet and black was white
When first this book was lent to me.

ENVOI

Princess, it's not at all polite
  To ask you for such history;
You were not in the world—not quite;
  When first this book was lent to me.

BALLADE OF THE MACKEREL-CATCHER

Crosswords are catching crowds untold,
  Wallace is catching crooks and spies,
The Adamites are catching cold,
  The Moslem Sheiks are catching—f-f-flies;

Selfridge is catching pumpkin-pies
To show them on a gilded dish,
  O. Nares is catching ladies' eyes
When Barbara is catching fish.

Stones at her touch would turn to gold
  And fish to goldfish, in such wise,
And sticklebacks change in her hold
  To sturgeons of enormous size.
  The detail need not cause surprise
(Clare will withdraw the expression "Pish!"),
  There is no need for telling lies
When Barbara is catching fish.

She of the Low-Backed Car of old[1]
  Made chickens' food for lovers' sighs,
What troops of Yanks through Lyme have rolled
  Envying this Fisher and her prize,
  Throngs of the Regularest Guys
All glog-glog-glog-glog-glog-gloggish,
  Uttering admiring "Gees!" and "Mys!"
When Barbara is catching fish.

ENVOI

  Princess, though eagles scale the skies,
It tempts me not: but how I wish
  I were a porpoise and could rise
When Barbara is catching fish.

BALLADE TO A PHILANTHROPIST

You send your ships to Sunlight Port,
  Your money to Morel and Co.,
Or the Minority Report
  Or the Maternity Bureau;

---

[1] If you don't know the song "Peggy in the Low-Backed Car", you ought
to. As she sat in her low-backed car/The lovers came from near and far/And
envied the chicken that Peggy was pickin'/As she sat in her low-backed car.
— G.K.C.

There is in all this festive flow
A point that I should like to fix,
   Your aid is shed on all below—
But will you lend me two-and-six?

You pay reformers to fall short,
   And agitators to lie low,
You pay our papers to exhort
   Our soldiers not to conquer so,
   You toss us a Town Hall at Bow
Built out of terra-cotta bricks—
   Has a Gymnasium, has it! Oh!
But will you lend me two-and-six?

I know you vetoed at Earl's Court
   That brutalising Billiard Show.
. . . Quite so . . . yes . . . yes . . . this so-called sport.
   Yes . . . so-called Christian . . . strikes a blow . . .
   Yes . . . so-called Twentieth . . . yes, I know,
. . . Degraded postures . . . player kicks
   The billiard-marker with his toe . . .
—*But will you lend me two-and-six?*

ENVOI

Prince, I will not be knighted! No!
Put up your sword and stow your tricks!
   Offering the Garter is no go—
BUT WILL YOU LEND ME TWO-AND-SIX?

A BALLADE OF CUTTING A STICK

I cut a cudgel under woods that lower,
   The deep dank woods where the last fairies sat,
Where lost and tangled is Titania's bower,
   'Mid darkness and the droning of the gnat,
   I seized a sapling, and so bent it that
With one long drag the deep roots came away,
   And the hills of the whole earth heaved and cried thereat;
I cut a cudgel in the woods to-day.

For lips of thunder moved in that mirk hour
    O'er all men evil that the earth begat,
The jerry-builder climbed his crazy tower,
    The brewer plunged into his poisoned vat;
    The Perfect Gentleman went mad and spat,
The Modern Preacher almost tried to pray,
    Lord Normantowers went home to Ballarat.
I cut a cudgel in the woods to-day.

I walked the London streets in sun and shower
    Behind a London banker, large and fat,
His faultless frock-coat had a faultless flower,
    His hat was high and black as any bat,
    Its silk was smooth; its top was bright and flat,
Its brim was curled in a peculiar way.
    —Ah Heaven! it was in dreams of such a hat
I cut a cudgel in the woods to-day.

ENVOI

    Prince, it is time we had a quiet chat
On Politics. . . . Come on, then, whack away!
    You have your golden sceptre—what of that?
I cut a cudgel in the woods to-day.

A BALLADE OF GREAT RIVERS

O you that dwell where city wharves are wet,
  Or choked with dust and cinders, soot and lime,
O you down by the Dockyards—I forget
  The place's name—or, as you call it, "nime,"
  In all your slavery and greed and grime—
You too may taste the earth's eternity,
  Hearing below bridges o'er the giant slime,
Returning rivers to the ancient sea.

And you that curse your cities, do not fret,
  These things shall vanish, and that voice sublime
Roar on by bolder boat and ruder net
  And merrier men that hear the morning chime,
  I say to you, though men be stewed in crime,
More as they once have been shall these things be.
  There is a noise in all the hills of time,
Returning rivers to the ancient sea.

Man, in his wits, shall yet return and set
  "Primary" education in its prime,
And Woman shall walk through the Suffragette,
  And God shall give us back the Pantomime;
  The Whitmanites are coming back to Rhyme,
The Pragmatists to Reason—cautiously—
  Returning pilgrims to a Christian clime,
Returning rivers to the ancient sea.

ENVOI

  Prince—is that you? Lorlumme! O Gorblime. . . .
(I too resume the speech of my degree)
  O crikey, Bill. . . . Lorluvaduck!—Well I'm—
Returning rivers to the ancient sea.

BALLADE OF A YOUNG LADY IN A HAMMOCK

You, wiser than the Queens of Care
    That in their ivory thrones have sat,
You have a hammock for a chair
    And wear a cushion for a hat;
    You have a net to catch the gnat
And Peter had a pole; and he
    Shall swing your vessel while you chat,
But swing it gently, Marjorie.

And we will talk of things that were
    When each and all were in a flat
Though Frances, in the gaudy glare
    Of her new garden, sneer thereat,
    Not I will scorn it, plot or plat,
With that broad sight of Battersea,
    And Room enough to swing a cat
(But swing it gently, Marjorie).

And frown not that he finds it fair,
    One so romantic and so fat
To find a modern woman there
    Quit of the modern tit-for-tat;
    Woman, we yield at once—*bis dat*—.
Career across the golfing tee,
    Swipe at us with the cricket bat—
But swing it gently, Marjorie.

ENVOI

Princess, I grovel on the mat:
Rock, rock (it is your destiny)
    The cradle—and the World at that—
But swing it gently, Marjorie.

THE BALLADE OF A STRANGE TOWN

Can Man to Mount Olympus rise,
  And fancy Primrose Hill the scene?
Can a man walk in Paradise
  And think he is in Turnham Green?
  And could I take you for Malines,
Not knowing the nobler thing you were?
  O Pearl of all the plain, and queen,
The lovely city of Lierre.

Through memory's mist in glimmering guise
  Shall shine your streets of sloppy sheen.
And wet shall grow my dreaming eyes,
  To think how wet my boots have been.
  Now if I die a Rural Dean,
Or rob a bank I do not care,
  Or turn a Tory. I have seen
The lovely city of Lierre.

Happy is he and more than wise
  Who sees with wondering eyes and clean
This world through all the grey disguise
  Of sleep and custom in between.
  Yes; we may pass the heavenly screen,
But shall we know when we are there?
  Who know not what these dead stones mean,
The lovely city of Lierre.

ENVOI

Prince, wide your Empire spreads, I ween,
Yet happier is that moistened Mayor,
  Who drinks her cognac far from *fine*,
The lovely city of Lierre.

A BALLADE OF DEAD MEN

Come, let us sit upon the grass
   And tell sad tales of human ill:
How Bacon was a silly ass
   Who caught a Chicken and a Chill;
   And Charles the First, who made his will
But managed to mislay his head;
   And Brown, who read the works of Mill,[1]
Who is unfortunately dead.

Queen Bess, who swore upon the Mass
   How many Catholics she'd kill;
Our glorious Marlborough, who, alas!
   Could not be trusted near the till;
   Chatham, who'd set the world a-thrill
And quite abruptly go to bed;
   And Tims, who took the 'Deathless' Pill,
Who is unfortunately dead.

Tales cling but fade; and falls the glass
   That Rosamunda failed to spill;
Faint rails the fragrance of the Lass
   Along the tiles of Richmond Hill:
   But Genesis is printed still,
And Homer's verses still are read—
   A writer of no little skill
Who is unfortunately dead.

[1] The philosopher, of whom Bentley wrote: John Stuart Mill,/By a mighty effort of will,/Overcame his natural bonhomie/And wrote "Principles of Political Economy."

Prince, pearls and diamonds, take your fill;
Don't mind if they are splashed with red:
   I got them from my poor Aunt Jill,
Who is unfortunately dead.

A BALLADE OF AN ANTI-PURITAN

They spoke of Progress spiring round
   Of Light and Mrs. Humphry Ward—
It is not true to say I frowned,
   Or ran about the room and roared:
   I might have simply sat and snored—
I rose politely in the club
   And said, "I feel a little bored;
Will some one take me to a pub?"

The new world's wisest did surround
   Me; and it pains me to record
I did not think their views profound,
   Or their conclusions well assured;
   The simple life I can't afford,
Besides, I do not like the grub,
   I want a mash and sausage, "scored"—
Will some one take me to a pub?

I know where men can still be found,
   Anger and clamorous accord,
And virtues growing from the ground,
   And fellowship of beer and board,
   And song, that is a sturdy cord,
And hope, that is a hardy shrub,
   And goodness, that is God's last word—
Will some one take me to a pub?

Prince, Bayard would have smashed his sword
To see the sort of knights you dub—
   Is that the last of them?—O Lord!
Will some one take me to a pub?

A BALLADE OF MONSTERS

"But cases of the kind are rare."– FROM
A MAGAZINE ARTICLE ON "CRIMINOLOGY."

A man has horns in Tufnell Park,
   A man eats clocks in Camberwell,
A man plays billiards in the dark
   Entirely by the sense of smell,
   A man I knew extremely well
Went up to bed and met a bear
   That said its name was "Little Nell":
But cases of the kind are rare.

A very shabby Clapham clerk
   Walked into the Savoy Hotel
With the stentorian remark
   That people there might go to hell.
   A duke, whose daughter cannot spell,
Was fined by the School Board at Ware,
   Brummell told George to ring the bell:
But cases of the kind are rare.

Then there were heroes: Joan of Arc,
   Nelson, of course, and William Tell,
And Johnny Phipps, who found a shark
   Inside his bath and didn't yell;
   And Lord Fitzowl, who wouldn't sell
His mother's bones to Mr. Maehr;
   And Blades who fought though Chartereds fell:
But cases of the kind are rare.

ENVOI

   Prince, princes lived who did Debell
Superbs and Subjects nobly spare,
   Who ruled their people really well,
But cases of the kind are rare.

BALLADE OF THE TEA-POT

Salt pork was sweet to Nelson's salted tar;
    Russians like train-oil tipped out of a can;
Petrol appears to please a motor-car,
    And potted greens a vegetarian.
    When the long lines of earnest brows I scan
Only one gastric certainty I see;
    In chapels chill and artists' parlours wan,
It is not well for men to live on tea.

I saw a man in wool who spoke on War.
    Peculiar ladies clapped when he began.
He dared in Dulwich to defy the Czar.
    He called the King 'our greatest Gentleman'.
    He said 'The flags of honour do but fan
Man's prehistoric animality.'
    But oh! Dan Chaucer—oh Dan—Dan—Dan,
It is not well for men to live on tea.

Be good, sweet maid; and follow that strong star
    Of sanity that lights our labouring clan;
Such things as thieving and blackmail I bar,
    And piracy I positively ban.
    Avoid assassination, if you can,
Don't be a slave to anthropophagy;
    It is not well for men to feed on man,
It is not well for men to live on tea.

ENVOI

    Prince, here's that everlasting Lady Ann,
Let's get our coats and cut our sticks and flee;
    Come round the corner to the 'Pig and Swan',
It is not well for men to live on tea.

TO FATHER O'CONNOR [1]

The scratching pen, the aching tooth,
　　The Plea for Higher Unity,
The aged buck, the earnest youth,
　　The Missing Link, the Busy Bee,
　　The Superman, the Third Degree,
Are things that I should greatly like
　　To take and sling quite suddenly
As far as Heaven from Heckmondwike;

As far as Hood is from Fitzooth,
　　As far as seraphs from a flea,
As far as Campbell from the truth,
　　Or old Bohemia from the sea
　　Or Shakespeare from Sir Herbert Tree
Or Nathan from an Arab Sheik
　　Or most of us from L.S.D.—
As far as Heaven from Heckmondwike;

As far as actresses from youth,
　　As far, as far as lunch from tea,
As far as Horton from Maynooth,
　　As far as Paris from Paree,
　　As far as Hawke is from a gee,
Or I am from an old high bike,
　　As far as Stead from Sanity,
As far as Heaven from Heckmondwike.

ENVOI

Prince, Cardinal that is to be,
Cardinals do not go on strike,
　　I'm far from wishing it (D.V.)
As far as Heaven from Heckmondwike.

---

[1] Inscribed in a copy of *The Ballad of the White Horse* presented to Father O'Connor

A BALLADE OF A STOIC

The griefs of friends how grave they often are!
    They've smashed my friend's five Titians in their frames.
My cousin broke three ribs beneath a car
    And had to pay for it in counter-claims;
    My mother's favourite chapel is in flames;
My father's best cashier is going blind;
    My niece is mad; my nephew's name is James;
My aunt is murdered—and I do not mind.

O cell where Socrates was like a star!
    O soul of Cato that no death defames!
The field where Montfort fell with many a scar;
    The gallows of the noblest of the Graemes;
    All these my larger virtue lops and lames
I am the Hero by the gods designed,
    The Stoic whom no lash of fortune tames.
My aunt is murdered—and I do not mind.

I had no hand in this distressing spar.
    When the assassin told me of his aims
I handed him a heavy iron bar
    And turned my back and watched the widening Thames.
    It's no good blaming me or calling names.
The Age of Chivalry is left behind;
    I don't profess to be a Squire of Dames.
My aunt is murdered—and I do not mind.

ENVOI

    Prince, what—in tears? Oh sight that shocks and shames!
Because the fifteenth housemaid has resigned,
    Come let us play those nice expensive games.
My aunt is murdered; and *I* do not mind.

LAST BALLADE[1]

The work of hoiking coal nuts from the mine,
  The work of shooting insects with a gun,
Of telling by the taste Good Wine from Wine
  With our strong toils compared are merely fun:
  To calculate the distance of the sun
Is not so hard—and what a time we've had!
  But that's all over now; the battle's won.
And you and I are infinitely glad.

The Bard of Ayrshire sang of Auld Lang Syne;
  The Bard of Avon made a brilliant pun;
The Bard of Thrace was helped by Muses Nine;
  The Bard of Old St. Paul's—his name was Donne—
  Wrote things which, if you read, you cannot run;
And Percy Shelley was a gifted lad.
  This is the last loud shrapnel from *our* gun.
And you and I are infinitely glad.

Byron described but never saw the Rhine.
  And Campbell sang but never fought the Hun.
Isaiah wrote when far from Palestine.
  Milton was blind. Carducci weighed a ton.
  Coleridge took opium. Homer took the bun.
And William Cowper wrote when he was mad.
  But we—no matter; it's the final one!
And you and I are infinitely glad.

ENVOI

  Prince, though they touch you up (and there was none,
That did not touch you up, however bad)
  The quarrel's settled, and our task is done.
And you and I are infinitely glad.

---

[1] By G.K.C. and Hilaire Belloc, Maurice Baring, J.S. Phillimore,
T. Michael Pope and Cecil Chesterton.

VII

...of Whom He Was Extremely Fond

Dedications and occasional verse

Pardon, dear Lady, if this Christmas time,
The Convalescent Bard in halting rhyme
Thanks you for that great thought that still entwines
The Wicked Grocer with more wicked lines;
These straggling Crayon lines—who cares for these,
Who knows the difference between Chalk and Cheese?

Not wholly sound the saw, accounted sure,
That weak things perish and strong things endure:
Milton, six volumes on my groaning shelves,
May groan till Judgement Day and please themselves
As, harsh with leaden type and leathery pride,
Puritan Bards must groan at Christmas tide:

My table groans with Stilton—for a while:
Paradise Found not Lost, in Milton's style
Green as his Eden; as his Michael strong:
But O, my friend, it will not groan there long.

DEDICATION OF *THE MAN WHO WAS THURSDAY*

TO EDMUND CLERIHEW BENTLEY

A cloud was on the mind of men, and wailing went the weather,
Yea, a sick cloud upon the soul when we were boys together.
Science announced nonentity and art admired decay;
The world was old and ended: but you and I were gay.
Round us in antic order their crippled vices came—
Lust that had lost its laughter, fear that had lost its shame.
Like the white lock of Whistler, that lit our aimless gloom,
Men showed their own white feather as proudly as a plume.
Life was a fly that faded, and death a drone that stung;
The world was very old indeed when you and I were young.
They twisted even decent sin to shapes not to be named:
Men were ashamed of honour; but we were not ashamed.
Weak if we were and foolish, not thus we failed, not thus;
When that black Baal blocked the heavens he had no hymns
      from us.
Children we were—our forts of sand were even as weak as we,
High as they went we piled them up to break that bitter sea.
Fools as we were in motley, all jangling and absurd,
When all church bells were silent our cap and bells were heard.

Not all unhelped we held the fort, our tiny flags unfurled;
Some giants laboured in that cloud to lift it from the world.
I find again the book we found, I feel the hour that flings
Far out of fish-shaped Paumanok some cry of cleaner things;
And the Green Carnation withered, as in forest fires that pass,
Roared in the wind of all the world ten million leaves of grass;
Or sane and sweet and sudden as a bird sings in the rain—
Truth out of Tusitala spoke and pleasure out of pain.
Yea, cool and clear and sudden as a bird sings in the grey,
Dunedin to Samoa spoke, and darkness unto day.
But we were young; we lived to see God break their bitter charms,
God and the good Republic come riding back in arms:
We have seen the City of Mansoul, even as it rocked, relieved—
Blessed are they who did not see, but being blind, believed.

This is a tale of those old fears, even of those emptied hells,
And none but you shall understand the true thing that it tells—
Of what colossal gods of shame could cow men and yet crash,

Of what huge devils hid the stars, yet fell at a pistol flash.
The doubts that were so plain to chase, so dreadful to withstand—
Oh, who shall understand but you; yea, who shall understand?
The doubts that drove us through the night as we two talked amain,
And day had broken on the streets e'er it broke upon the brain.
Between us, by the peace of God, such truth can now be told;
Yea, there is strength in striking root, and good in growing old.
We have found common things at last, and marriage and a creed,
And I may safely write it now, and you may safely read.

DEDICATION OF *THE NAPOLEON OF NOTTING HILL*
TO HILAIRE BELLOC

For every tiny town or place
God made the stars especially;
Babies look up with owlish face
And see them tangled in a tree:
You saw a moon from Sussex Downs,
A Sussex moon, untravelled still,
I saw a moon that was the town's,
The largest lamp on Campden Hill.

Yea; Heaven is everywhere at home,
The big blue cap that always fits,
And so it is (be calm; they come
To goal at last, my wandering wits),
So is it with the heroic thing;
This shall not end for the world's end,
And though the sullen engines swing,
Be you not much afraid, my friend.

This did not end by Nelson's urn
Where an immortal England sits—
Nor where your tall young men in turn
Drank death like wine at Austerlitz.
And when the pedants bade us mark
What cold mechanic happenings
Must come; our souls said in the dark,
'Belike; but there are likelier things.'

Likelier across these flats afar
These sulky levels smooth and free
The drums shall crash a waltz of war
And Death shall dance with Liberty;
Likelier the barricades shall blare
Slaughter below and smoke above,
And death and hate and hell declare
That men have found a thing to love.

Far from your sunny uplands set
I saw the dream; the streets I trod,
The lit straight streets shot out and met
The starry streets that point to God.
This legend of an epic hour
A child I dreamed, and dream it still,
Under the great grey water-tower
That strikes the stars on Campden Hill.

HECKMONDWIKE[1]

This is a book I do not like
Take it away to Heckmondwike—
A lurid exile, lost and sad,
To punish it for being bad.
You need not take it from the shelf
(I tried to read it once myself:
The speeches jerk, the chapters sprawl,
The story makes no sense at all);
Hide it your Yorkshire moors among
Where no man speaks the English tongue.

Hail, Heckmondwike! Successful spot!
Save from the Latin's festering lot,
Where Horton and where Hocking see
The grace of heaven, Prosperity,
Above the chimneys hung and bowed
A pillar of most solid cloud;

[1] Inscribed in a book for Father O'Connor.

To starved oppressed Italian Eyes
The place would seem a paradise,
And many a man from Como Lake
And many a Tyrolese would take
(If Priests allowed them what they like)
Their holidays in Heckmondwike.

The Belgian with his bankrupt woes
Who through deserted Brussels goes,
The Rind that threads those ruins bare
Where Munich and where Milan were
Hears owls and wolves like Gehenna
In the best quarters of Vienna;
It murmurs in tears "Ah how unlike
The happiness of Heckmondwike!"

In Spain the sad guitar they strike
And yearning, sing of Heckmondwike;
The Papal Guard leans on his pike
And dreams he is in Heckmondwike;
Peru's proud horsemen long to bike
But for one hour in Heckmondwike;
Offered a Land Bill, Pat and Mike
Cry "Give us stones—in Heckmondwike!"
Bavarian beer is good, belike,
But try the gin of Heckmondwike;
The Flamands drown in ditch and dyke
Their itch to be in Heckmondwike,
Rise Freedom, with the sword to strike!
And turn the world to Heckmondwike.

Take then, this book I do not like—
It may improve in Heckmondwike.

[AN APOLOGY FOR NOT WRITING]

He thought he saw the Unicorn, the horned and holy horse,
He looked again and saw it was a Subject for Remorse:
He rushed for what he meant to post—
                    and didn't post, of course.

He thought he saw the Unicorn, the Virgin's wildest pet,
He looked again and saw it was a Long Outstanding Debt.
He wrote and wrote and wrote and wrote—
                              and hasn't written yet.

He thought he saw the Unicorn, her mane a wind of pride,
He looked again and tried again, and worked until he died;
He ordered a Pantechnicon—
                              that's waiting still outside.

He thought he saw the Unicorn, that breaketh curb and bond,
He looked and saw a girl of whom he was extremely fond . . .
The floods rose to the Chilterns when
                              they found him in his pond.

He thought he saw the Unicorn, crowned of the Silver Spear,
He wondered if it was a Stag and saw it was a Dear—
And so he drowned himself—
                              some say in Water—
                                        some in Beer.

TRUE SYMPATHY
or
PREVENTION OF CRUELTY TO TEACHERS

I was kind to all my masters
    And I never worked them hard
To goad them to exactitude
    Or speaking by the card.

If one of them should have the air
    Of talking through his hat
And call a curve isosceles
    I let it go at that.

The point was without magnitude;
    I knew without regret
Our minds were moving parallel
    Because they never met.

Because I could not bear to make
    An Algebraist cry
I gazed with interest at x
    And never thought of Why.

That he should think I thought he thought
    That x was ABC
Was far, far happier for him
    And possibly for me.

While other teachers raved and died
    In reason's wild career,
Men who had driven themselves mad
    By making themselves clear,

My teachers laugh and sing and dance,
    Aged, but still alive;
Because I often let them say
    That two and two are five.

Angles obtuse appeared acute,
    Angles acute were quite
Obtuse; but I was more obtuse:
    Their angles were all right.

I wore my Soul's Awakening smile
    I felt it was my duty:
Lo! Logic works by Barbara
    And life is ruled by Beauty.

I am now ten years old.

And Mathematics merged and met
   Its Higher Unity,
Where Five and Two and Twelve and Four
   They all were One to me.

LINES TO WATERLOO STATION
AN OVERFLOWING OF FEELING

Come hither, Fisher Unwin
   And leave your work awhile,
Uplooking in my face a span
   With bright adoring smile.
All happy leaping Publishers
   Round Paternoster Row,
Gay Simpkin, dreamy Marshall
   And simple Sampson Low,
Come round, forgetting all your fears,
   Your hats and dinners too,
While I remark with studied calm,
   "Hurrah for Waterloo!"

Nay start not, fearful Putnam,
   I sing no warrior's fall
(Macmillan, smile again and dry
   The tears of Kegan Paul)
But seldom on the spot I sing
   Is heard the peal of guns,
Men do not charge for batteries
   They only charge for buns,
No chief expires, no trumpet
   I blow, except my own,
But harmless season tickets
   Expire without a groan.

I've been in all the waiting-rooms
   I never chanced to see
An army: but observant
   I never claimed to be—
If someone through my body drove
   A bayonet like a spit

I listened to Miss Frances Blogg
    And did not notice it.

Yet still thy Gladstone bags shall woo
    Thy labels' bashful kiss
Geologists shall reconcile
    Thy cake with Genesis,

(Here the page ends—and with it all
that remains of the poem.)

MASTERMAN AND CHESTERTON

Lo: Masterman and Chesterton
    This happy picture shows.
The former is the one whose eye
With a fine pathos glows.
    I am the one with auburn hair
And the finely chiselled nose.

Thus between heaven and earth they passed
    Over the Kentish plain.
The earth was noble English mud,
The heavens were mostly rain.
    If you should see their faces, you
Will know them both again.

HISTORY OF THE HUSBANDS OF RHODA

These suitors rolled upon the sand.
Asking for Rhoda's heart and hand.

(1) Professor Piff, whose "Tuscan Rome"
Is loved in every English home
Bits from his "British Trace in Gaul"
Bring down the house at the music hall.

(2) Roy Beauchamp, you observe to follow
A god, an artist, an Apollo—
What little Cash, I am aware,
He had to spare, he did not spare.

(3) Sbolsky: an Anarchist, still alive:
Politically known as "5".
He blew up thousands, it was said.
Married and was blown up instead.

(4) Through Major Bumper's pleasant oaths
Moustaches, and delightful clothes
He was M.P. for Gallowglass.
To represent the working class——.

(5) Giles Rosethorn was an actor free
Who with romantic mystery
Buttoned that cape about his throat
Because he had not got a Coat.

(6) And Mimmer! Music he in sum!
    He played the fiddle, fife and drum
    He played the fool, when all was spent,
    It was his favourite instrument.

(7) Good Captain Cubby then began,
    A fine old country gentleman,
    With him our Rhoda lived at ease
    Perpetually shelling peas.—

(8) Then came the Rev. Ehud Boe
    ("The Battle-Blast of Pimlico")
    He turned a Mormon later on
    And married ten. But One had gone.

(9) Living with Philip William Trevor
    One had no sentiments whatever.

(10 Swarra Na Gulosnaphyaptarwadkz
    which, let me tell you, rhymes to "boots"
    His ways were somewhat savage: he
    Ate his papa . . . but reverently.

(11) Of Colonel Brown.—
         the writer begs,
    To utter nothing but the legs.

A CURSE IN FREE VERSE

(This is the only rhyme admitted: otherwise the enchanting lyric
is all that the most fastidious fashionable taste could require):

I CURSE PARADOX—
I curse the contradictory inconsistencies of the Modern Mind:
I curse and curse and curse . . .

Those who dogmatise about the folly of dogma:
Those who moralise about the non-existence of morals:
Those who say people are too stupid to educate their children
But not too stupid to educate each other's:
Those who say we can be certain of nothing.
Because we are so certain of all the exploded evolutionary
   hypotheses
That show we can be certain of nothing . . .
But what are all these inconsistencies—
Compared with the conduct of Those Who
Deliberately Call Their House Christmas Cottage,
And then go away from it at Christmas?

I hate those who wage and win twenty unjust wars
And then say "The World now requires Peace",
Who then make a League for Peace and use it to make
  another War:
I hate those who intemperately denounce Beer and call it
  Temperance;
Those who deny what science says about Cancer
And what Christianity says about Calvary
And Call the Contradiction Christian Science.
I hate those who want to Rise out of Barbarism
By running about naked and grubbing up roots and herbs;
But what are all these aversions . . .?
Compared with the blighting blistering horror and hatred
With which I regard
THOSE WHO CALL THEIR HOUSE CHRISTMAS
COTTAGE AND THEN GO AWAY FROM IT AT
CHRISTMAS?

(The Poet is removed, cursing . . .)

THE CHRISTIAN SOCIAL UNION

The Christian Social Union here
Was very much annoyed;
It seems there is some duty
Which we never should avoid,
And so they sang a lot of hymns
To help the Unemployed.

Upon a platform at the end
The speakers were displayed
And Bishop Hoskins stood in front
And hit a bell and said
That Mr. Carter was to pray,
And Mr. Carter prayed.

Then Bishop Gore of Birmingham
He stood upon one leg
And said he would be happier
If beggars didn't beg,
And that if they pinched his palace
It would take him down a peg.

He said that Unemployment
Was a horror and a blight,
He said that charities produced

Servility and spite,
And stood upon the other leg
And said it wasn't right.

And then a man named Chesterton
Got up and played with water,
He seemed to say that principles
Were nice and led to slaughter
And how we always compromised
And how we didn't orter.

Then Canon Holland fired ahead
Like fifty cannons firing,
We tried to find out what he meant
With infinite enquiring,
But the way he made the windows jump
We couldn't help admiring.

I understood him to remark
(It seemed a little odd)
That half a dozen of his friends
Had never been in quod.
He said he was a Socialist himself,
And so was God.

He said the human soul should be
Ashamed of every sham,
He said a man should constantly
Ejaculate "I am."
When he had done, I went outside
And got into a tram.

TO ENID, WHO ACTED THE CAT IN PRIVATE PANTOMIME

Though cats and birds be hardly friends,
   We doubt the Maeterlinckian word
That must dishonour the White Cat,
   Even to honour the Blue Bird.

And if once more in later days
  His baseless charge the Belgian brings,
Great ghosts shall rise to vindicate
  The right of cats to look at kings.

The Lord of Carabas shall come
  In gold and ermine, silk and furs,
To tell of that immortal cat
  That wore its boots and won its spurs.

Great Whittington shall show again
  The state that London lends her Lord,
Where the great golden griffins bear
  The blazon of the cross and sword.

And hear the ancient bells anew,
  And talk and not ignobly brag
What glorious fortunes followed when
  He let the cat out of the bag.

And Gray shall leave the graves of Stoke
  To weep over a gold-fish bowl—
Cowper, who, beaming at his cat,
  Forgot the shadow on his soul.

Then shall I rise and name aloud
  The nicest cat I ever knew,
And make the fairy fancies pale
  With half a hundred tales of you:

Till Pasht upon his granite throne
   Glare with green eyes to hear the news,
Jealous; and even Puss in Boots
   Will wish that he were in your shoes.

When I shall pledge in saucers full
   Of milk, on which the kitten thrives,
Feline felicities to you
   And nine extremely prosperous lives.

WE ARE NOT AMUSED

Puck and the woodland elves shall weep with me
For that lost joke I made in Ledborough Lane,
The joke that Mrs. Baines declined to see
Although I made it very loud and plain.
I made the joke again and yet again,
I analysed it, parsed it and explained:
I did my very best to entertain,
But Mrs. Baines would not be entertained.

FOLK SONG[1]

Six detectives went fishing
   Down by the sea-side.
They found a Dead Body
   And enquired how it died.

Father Brown he informed them
   Quite mild, and without scorn:
'Like you and me and the rest of us,
   He died of being born.'

The Detective from the Daily News
   Asked 'Where are the Dead?'
And Father Brown coughed gently
   And he answered and said

'If you'll come to St Cuthbert's
   I'll tell you today.'
But the other Five Detectives
   Went weeping away.

TO YOUNG PESSIMISTS

Some sneer; some snigger; some simper;
In the youth where we laughed, and sang.
And *they* may end with a whimper
But *we* will end with a bang.

---

[1] Inscribed in a copy of *The Secret of Father Brown* presented to Father O'Connor.

INDEX OF TITLES